POLICE
EQUIPMENT

POLICE EQUIPMENT

Andy Bucholz

THUNDER BAY
P·R·E·S·S

This edition published by
Thunder Bay Press
5880 Oberlin Drive, Suite 400
San Diego, California 92121
1-800-284-3580

http://www.advmkt.com

Produced by
PRC Publishing Ltd,
Kiln House, 210 New Kings Road, London SW6 4NZ

ISBN 1 57145 157 9

1 2 3 4 5 98 99 00 01 02

Printed and bound in China

Acknowledgements
All the photographs for this book were kindly provided by Andy Bucholz.
Specific photographers have been credited underneath the relevant captions.
The publisher gratefully acknowledges the assistance of Simon Clay, who provided the
photography for the following pages:

1, 2-3, 6, 7, 8-9 (main), 8 (inset), 9 (inset), 13 (both), 28, 38, 41 (both), 50 (inset),
52 (inset), 55 (bottom), 58 (top left), 70 (both), 71 (all), 72 (both), 73 (both), 74 (all),
77 (all), 80 (all), 83 (top, middle and bottom right), 100 (both), 102 (top), 106 (inset),
107 (inset), 109, 116, 123 (inset), 131 and 137.

**Page 1: This NYPD badge, in use in 1857-70, shows how a number was used to tie a
particular officer to a badge so he could be traced. Around the shield are the words
"Metropolitan Police" relating to the fact that it was a city police force.**

**Page 2: A more traditional color scheme of black and white is employed by Long Beach
for their patrol cars. Whatever markings are employed it will always be uniform
throughout the fleet of vehicles and readily identifiable, so that even somebody from out
of state will recognize the vehicle as a police car.**

Contents

INTRODUCTION

Modern Law Enforcement

The first civilizations formed by man used military force to keep the peace. Since the people were mostly agrarian in nature, either farming or tending animals, crime like we know it did not exist. Members of a community dealt with community criminals internally and used the military to solve crimes committed by people outside of the community. As human population increased so did the size of cities. This led to the creation of the nightwatch to patrol areas. The nightwatch were similar to our modern neighborhood watch in that they were not specifically trained for law enforcement duties. The watch was normally made up of all able-bodied men that were generally unpaid for their efforts.

The policy of having unpaid watchmen lasted until 1749 when the Philadelphia legislature passed a law creating a tax to pay for full-time watchmen. The new full-time watchmen had increased duties and more powers of arrest to prevent and control crime. Philadelphia felt there was a need to hire full-time watchmen to combat what was possibly the first crime wave know to modern civilization. The Industrial Revolution caused a large number of the rural population to relocate to central urban districts in order to seek employment. The new urban areas created many opportunities but also led to a dramatic increase in criminal opportunities. This type of population boom created the first crime waves that the

Right: Just down the road from Chicago, in Oak Park, officers rely less on markings and more on the bar light to identify the vehicle.

Left: This shot shows an officer going out on patrol complete with a radio attached to his tooled leather belt, which these days also carries additional extras in pouches such as sprays and handcuffs.

Right: The signs on the garage door tell you this is home to No. 1 squad situated next to the 13th Precinct on 21st Street, Lower Manhattan and covering the most diverse of all the areas. It is affectionately known as the "Hollywood Truck" thanks to all the media exposure gained while on the job.

world had ever seen. The watchmen of the past could not control the crime that was taking place. Although population in the cities was booming then, it wasn't anything like what it would be in the years to come. For instance, New York City grew from 60,000 people in 1800 to 4,000,000 people by 1900.

Great Britain, which was more industrialized than the U.S. at the time, had larger cities and more crime problems. In 1829, in London, the first professional crime prevention police department was created. In order to stand apart from the military they chose a blue coat, blue pants and a black hat. This was the first men in blue. It wasn't until 1844 in the U.S. that New York started the first crime prevention police department.

The New York City police officer was very different than those of today. First, they wore no uniform and were required to only wear a badge and secondly they were not allowed to carry a firearm. Americans at the time were very worried about having an armed and uniformed police force since

Top left: The big rescue unit, an '86 Ford Truck built by Salisbury, with the left hand side showing how the exterior opens to reveal various compartments containing different types of equipment.

Left: Two officers wait by their cruiser while responding to a non-emergency call.

POLICE EQUIPMENT

Right, top to bottom: Here we see a routine arrest, the officer first restrains two suspects, cuffs their wrists, then puts one on the ground to cuff one's ankles.

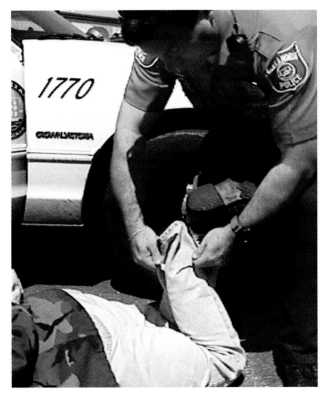

they saw any man in uniform with the power to arrest as tyrannical and subversive to the free American lifestyle.

Even today, Americans argue about how much power the police are allowed to have. Perceptions of a "Police State" where police oppress citizens is always being balanced against the rights of criminals and due process. It soon became apparent to the citizens of New York in the middle 1800s that the police department had to have a uniform so that people could recognize them and their presence would serve as a crime deterrent.

At this same time Americans were starting to move west in ever increasing numbers. Border States with the west were often sparsely populated and law enforcement was usually non-existent or inexperienced. The west posed a much different task for law enforcement since criminals would often commit a crime and then flee into the Territories where they could not be extradited. The new States were bordered by vast Federal Territory dotted with Indian land (reservations and territory). U.S. Marshals had jurisdiction in Federal Territory, while Indian Territory was often lawless.

After the Civil War gold and silver were discovered in the west which brought thousands of people together to form towns and cities without any standardized government assistance. The train linked up the east of the U.S. with the west and innovations with the gun and bullet made firearms cheap and reliable. The combination of plentiful firearms, lots of money generated from the gold rush, and the chaos of no or limited uniform law enforcement made for the wild west that movies and literature has romantized. Of course, the real west was not like the movies but there is a lot of truth used in the fiction.

Police Departments of the early 20th century still had a long way to go before they could be considered a modern police force. This was true because Police Departments still did not have a uniform method for evidence gathering neither did they have a technique to identify criminals.

Fictional sleuths like Sherlock Holmes solved cases using intelligence and observation which police of the 1880's had to rely on since uniform evidence gathering and criminalistics had not been invented yet.

CHAPTER ONE
Weapons

CHAPTER ONE

Handguns

*"Most officers who are killed by felonious action
are killed at zero to 10 feet."*

One of the main goals for each individual officer is to protect and serve their community. However, they also want to leave work in one piece. Sometimes officers have problems with suspects that turn violent or resist a lawful arrest. The use of force by officers is strictly regulated. Officers are allowed to use force when they are effecting an arrest, overcoming resistance, preventing an escape, defending their person, or defending the general public. Furthermore, the force used must be reasonable based on

the facts and circumstances known to the officer at the time force is used. There are many other factors that an officer must evaluate to determine what kind of force is necessary to either effect an arrest or stop the suspect's aggressive actions. These rules of engagement are established to help officers judge which action to take in defending themselves or others.

Basically, if an unarmed suspect wants to fight with his bare hands to prevent being lawfully arrested, the officer is not required

Right: Officers train for hours so that they can act instinctively when the situation calls for deadly force. Here a police officer fires from the Weaver stance, which is a two-handed support position. *Photograph courtesy of Leslie O'Shaughnessy Studios*

to keep the status quo and fight the suspect with his hands. The goal of the officer is not to fight a suspect but to make an arrest and therefore he or she would be authorized to escalate the use of force to using the baton or pepper spray in order to subdue the suspect. On the other hand, if the suspect were then to produce a knife, club, or other lethal weapon the officer would then be justified in escalating the use of force to a gun. Determining whether the force used is reasonable requires a careful balancing of factors including, but not limited to, the probable severity of injury to officers, suspects and others as a result of the application of force.

To this end, the use of deadly force is the last resort for an officer and is a very serious part of the job that requires a lot of decision-making training. For the most part, police departments determine which type of hand gun that the jurisdiction will use, whether that is a revolver or a self-loader (automatic). All of the officers in the department are then issued the same type of weapon. Standardization has many purposes; one weapon means there will be only one type of ammunition needed; it is easier and cost effective to train all officers the same way; and in a crisis officers can use each other's ammunition and or handgun.

More and more jurisdictions are switching to the large-magazine-capacity self-loading handguns (automatic) in replacement of the revolver. This is because the self-loader has proven itself reliable and can hold more bullets than a revolver. Simply put, a revolver holds six bullets and a self-loader typically holds 15 in the magazine and one in the chamber. The additional number of bullets can make all the difference especially when criminals are arming themselves with better and more powerful weapons. For instance, 20 years ago a typical firearm used by criminals was the "Saturday Night Special" which was a .32/.38 caliber revolver that held five or six bullets. Now, the most common firearm is a 9mm self-loader that can hold 16 bullets.

When handguns were first used by law enforcement the revolver was the only type available. It was widely taught many years ago that the fastest most accurate handgun firing technique was the draw to the hip. Like the Wild West, the lawmen of the day

Left: This handgun is fitted with a pressure activated flashlight to aid the officer in locating suspects in low light environments. The pressure switch is on the handle and the wire connects it to the flashlight.

Below Left: Here is a standard "six-shot," revolver. Notice the leather strap that fits over the hammer of the handgun. This strap helps keep the weapon from falling out accidentally and also helps deter suspects from taking it.

learned to draw and fire their weapon like gunfighters. This outdated technique has been set aside for the two handed firing stance, called the Weaver stance, that had the officer draw the weapon up to where his eyes could better aim the handgun while his non-firing hand cupped the bottom of his first hand to provide a steadier position.

Officers learn that most armed confrontations with suspects will be at a very close range with 85% of officer related shootouts being within seven yards. This type of close range shooting leaves little time to react so the officer must be well prepared to deal with these types of close confrontations. Training provides a vital role in the

POLICE EQUIPMENT

"The 9mm semi-automatic was the most popular type of local police sidearm, with 69% of departments authorizing its use by officers." Bureau of Justice Statistics.

preparedness of the officer. Officers normally spend two weeks learning how to properly aim, shoot, and reload their duty handgun and standard shotgun with refresher courses every six months. This training includes shooting at night; firing from standing, kneeling, and prone positions; and to draw their gun and fire while lying on their back.

A common training reminder that new officers get is that in every confrontation there will be at least one handgun present — yours. Suspects will often try to wrestle the officer's handgun away and use it against the officer. Holsters used by police have retention systems designed to keep the gun in the holster and prevent it from falling out or being easily pulled out. Officers learn to draw their weapon in a special way that allows them to work with the retention system yet draw just as quickly.

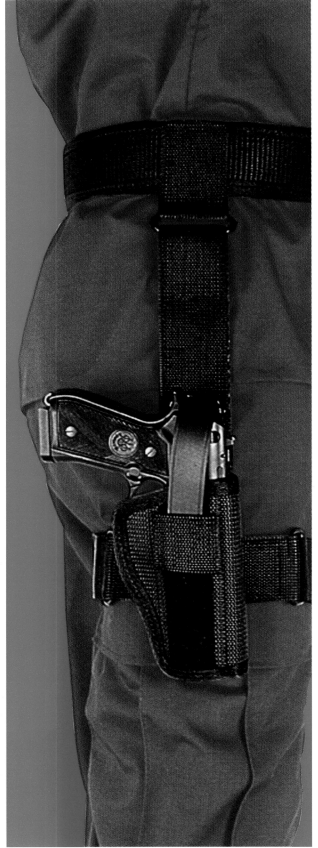

Right: Officers often carry back-up weapons like knives and handguns in case of emergency. Most back-up handguns are small and can be concealed in the officer's pant legs for quick access. *Photograph courtesy of Gould & Goodrich*

Far Right: K-9, SWAT, and other special police units often need more room at belt level for other items so they carry their service handgun lower on the hip. *Photograph courtesy of Gould & Goodrich*

Left: Officers practice using their handguns on an obstacle course where targets must be identified and hit while on the move. *Photograph courtesy of the Sure-Fire Institute*

CHAPTER ONE

Shotguns

Below Right: A hidden switch with a time delay allows the officer to continue driving to an emergency and take the shotgun out of the secure rack at the same time. Note that the officer does not have to look for the shotgun so he can keep his eyes focused on the real problems. *Photograph courtesy of Big Sky Racks, Inc.*

Far Right: In order to be proficient with the shotgun, officers practice firing during the day, at night, and as they move through obstacle courses. *Photograph courtesy of the Sure-Fire Institute*

The handgun is not always enough firepower for the dangerous situations that police find themselves. The 12-gauge shotgun is employed to help officers perform their jobs and add a large dose of firepower to the scene. The shotgun differs from a rifle because the barrel is smooth and has no rifling. When slug ammunition is used the slug will be rifled to provide better accuracy for the round.

The standard shotgun that thousands of officers carry with them in their cruisers daily is a direct descendant of the bird hunting shotgun used to hunt for food and protect early American settlers of the west. The early western law man and stagecoach guards incorporated the shotgun into law enforcement applications. They carried the shotgun for the same reason modern day officers use them; nothing beats a shotgun for close range stopping power. A blast from a shotgun at close range (closer than 20 feet) will change the physical condition of a suspect since the buckshot does not have time to spread out it creates a massive tunnel through the target. At a medium distance the buckshot will spread out and hit more tissue simultaneously creating a better chance of system failure. At a distance of 100 yards, the officer would need to use a slug because buckshot will have spread too far out to reach the target.

POLICE EQUIPMENT

Above: This is a clear view of the pressure activated light switch for the shotgun. *Photograph courtesy of the Sure-Fire Institute*

Above Right: In an armed conflict officers try to show as little of themselves as possible to be the least amount of target for the suspect. *Photograph courtesy of the Sure-Fire Institute*

Right:The shotgun this officer holds has a pistol grip with a rifle type sights and six extra shotgun shells for quick reloading. *Photograph courtesy of the Sure-Fire Institute*

Armed combat is much different for a police officer than it is for someone in the military. To win in a military confrontation one needs rapid and sustained firepower. For police officers, they will mostly encounter one or two armed suspects where the idea is to get at least one shot on target as quickly as possible to win. The shotgun can deliver a massive amount of firepower quickly and with few exceptions stop the aggressive actions of a suspect.

Just because the shotgun has more firepower does not mean the officer wants to pull it out for every situation. Most suspects offer no resistance when being arrested and it is hard to do any other law enforcement activities, like putting handcuffs on a suspect, while wielding a shotgun. The shotgun can be a liability since it cannot be put in a holster like the sidearm. Another issue concerning shotguns is using it in a crowd since the buckshot from a shotgun is not as accurate at long ranges as a handgun.

Left: The shotgun has a deep psychological effect on a suspect and is especially useful in providing cover. *Photograph courtesy of the Sure-Fire Institute*

CHAPTER ONE

Submachine Guns & Assault Rifles

Not every officer carries a submachine gun or assault rifle since these special weapons are not necessary for most street patrol activities. Only certain officers and SWAT teams will have the use of these particular weapons. Unlike pistols or shotguns the submachine gun and assault rifle have different settings for the rate of fire. These two types of weapons can be set to fire one bullet at a time, two/three bullets at a time, or full automatic. There may be some confusion as to handguns that are called automatic and the submachine gun's automatic capability. The self-loading, magazine fed handgun is only an automatic when in contradistinction to the revolver. But this handgun is really only semi-automatic since the trigger must be pulled each time the user wants the weapon to fire. Whereas, the submachine gun is a true automatic (often called full automatic) because the weapon can continue to fire as long as the trigger is depressed. A submachine gun is a machine gun that fires pistol ammuni-

Right: Submachine guns provide a lot of firepower for a small unit of police. In this photo the standing officer is using an assault rifle manufactured by Colt while the middle officer uses a Heckler & Koch made submachine gun.
Photograph courtesy of 21st Century Hard Armor Protection, Inc.

tion and an assault rifle is a machine gun (may be made to fire only semi-automatic also) that fires larger rifle ammunition in an automatic fashion.

Modern law enforcement is currently dealing with the problem started with drugs like crack cocaine giving common drug gangs access to lots of money. Wars over the location (turf) to sell these drugs made these criminals want to arm themselves. New handguns and submachine guns had been developed in the 1970s and 80s that made these weapons smaller, more reliable, and cheaper. Supply of weapons met demand for them leading to the U.S. murder rate soaring in the late 80s and early 90s. Because officers encounter suspects wielding extremely powerful weapons it generates a kind of arms race for police departments to keep up with what is being used on the street. Drug dealers fighting over turf and drug addicts robbing people for the money to buy these drugs made guns more common on the street.

The prevalence of guns on the streets and this gun lifestyle changed the way some people interacted with each other. A fight in school that would have been with fists twen-ty years ago would often be resolved with a gun, while things like drive-by shootings were becoming part of our vocabulary. Police jurisdictions all across America reported an upswing in the confiscation of guns of greater firepower, as measured by magazine capacity and rate of fire (full auto-matic) during the last several years.

Recently there was a bank robbery in Los Angeles California that was perpetrated by two men armed with full automatic assault rifles and dressed from head to toe in body armor. The first several dozen police that responded to the scene were armed only with their service handguns and shotguns. These weapons did not penetrate the many levels of body armor the suspects were wearing yet the bullets the suspects were fir-ing were tearing holes through cruisers, innocent civilians, and police. It was not until police began arming themselves with more powerful weapons that the suspects were stopped. Because of the courage of the responding police officers no one but the suspects died in the situation but the evi-dence was clear across the country that police had better keep up in the arms race with the modern criminal.

Below: This SWAT officer holds an assault rifle that is equipped with a flashlight up front and a scope on top. He has a radio head-set on his ear to talk to dispatch and the other officers in the SWAT team. *Photograph courtesy of the Sure-Fire Institute*

Right: This SWAT officer uses a laser-aiming device atop the submachine gun that puts a red dot on the target. This type of aiming device can improve shooter confidence and the accuracy of the weapon. *Photograph courtesy of Aimpoint, Inc.*

Far Right, Top: This SWAT team moves to clear a warehouse and the lead officer carries an assault rifle while the other officers use shotguns. *Photograph courtesy of the Sure-Fire Institute*

Far Right, Below: This officer provides cover while using his cruiser for concealment. *Photograph courtesy of Heckler & Koch, Inc.*

CHAPTER ONE

Rifles

Below Right: This SWAT sniper has positioned himself on a rooftop so that he can have the best view of the situation. One role of the SWAT sniper is to provide cover for the entry team and if the situation were to become potentially fatal he will shoot to protect the lives of the others.
Photograph courtesy of the San Francisco Police Department

Far Right: Police snipers normally shoot from great distances (average 70 yards) so another officer called the spotter assists in determining target(s). *Photograph courtesy of Aimpoint, Inc.*

Most patrol officers have ready access to shotguns when they feel they need more firepower than their service handgun. The shotgun has been with law enforcement for a very long time and as officers will attest; traditions die-hard. A number of police departments are trying rifles for a back-up weapon. Gun manufacturers are making carbines that are short and handy for police patrol purposes. These weapons are precise with minimal recoil, which makes the recovery quicker and faster for the officer to reacquire the target. The police rifle is more accurate than a shotgun at a distance. For crowded cities the police rifle can be a better option than using a shotgun because of the scatter affect of the shotgun.

SWAT teams also use a rifle but this weapon is not for regular patrol use. The SWAT sniper rifle is a special weapon for one user and one purpose. The purpose of a police sniper is to place one well-aimed shot in order to bring a critical life-threatening situation to a conclusion. The police sniper has one of the most pressure filled jobs law enforcement can offer other than the bomb squad. The police sniper must be prepared to neutralize a suspect with one precisely placed bullet that will immediately end all voluntary muscle activity. Only an exact shot to a suspect's neural motor strips (brain stem) will stop a suspect from being able to pull a trigger or cut a throat after he has been shot. There is little room for error since this area of the brain is no bigger than a baseball and the average distance to the target is 70 yards.

This type of precise shooting requires the officer to be very familiar with his rifle since no two fire exactly the same. Each police sniper is issued his own rifle that they will use exclusively. Officers are encouraged to practice firing their weapon under different conditions like day/night, wind/no wind, and summer/winter to fully understand the complexities of their task and the rifle they use to accomplish this task.

Police snipers use high-powered scopes to help them as well as other more high-tech gadgets like infrared lasers, tritium inserts, and holographic imaging devices. A sniper also receives some low-tech assistance from another officer called a spotter. These officers sit next to the police sniper with a spotting scope to ensure correct identification of the target and to help interface with the officer-in-charge of the situation.

Left and inset: Police Snipers will often take a position for several hours as they wait for an incident to be rendered safe. For these long waits the officers often take mats (often bullet-resistant) to lay on. *Photographs courtesy of Heckler & Koch, Inc.*

Below: For accuracy, a SWAT sniper and spotter, will both keep a close eye on their target.

CHAPTER ONE

Mace & Tear Gas

Right: Here is a close up of a can of pepper spray. Pepper spray is sold in some states to civilians at a 2% pepper mixture. Park rangers use 10% pepper mixture to fend off bears while police use 5% pepper mixture.

The world's military forces throughout history have used chemical weapons. People have been poisoning wells of besieged cities or catapulting deceased bodies over the walls of their enemies for many centuries. Even in our current history the armies that fought in World War I used mustard gas and other chemical agents to incapacitate or kill their enemy.

Non-lethal chemical weapons first saw widespread use during the Vietnam War era. Orthochlorobenzalmalonitrile (CS), or tear gas, was used to deny the enemy large areas of territory in Vietnam. On the homefront, the U.S. military and police were using tear gas as a way to break up riots throughout the country in such places as Detroit, Watts, and Kent State.

Tear gas comes in a crystalline form and mixes with air which produce fumes that causes a burning and choking sensation. Tear gas is slow acting and can take 10 to 30 seconds to start its reaction. The intended function of tear gas is to be distributed over a large area in order to prevent unprotected individuals access to the area. Tear gas is most effective in a riot situation where the authorities want to disperse a crowd from gathering and continuing aggressive action. Police typically hand throw a grenade or fire a grenade using a grenade launcher to deliver tear gas.

During this same time another version of tear gas was introduced, alphachloroacetaphenone (CN), or mace tear gas. Although mace tear gas was weaker in its affects on people than CS tear gas, it was much quicker to take affect. Mace tear gas only takes 3 to 10 seconds to start its

reaction. This made mace tear gas a better buy for the self-defense market than CS tear gas. Individual containers that can be hand held and sprayed at one person or a group of people made mace tear gas popular for the police officer on patrol. Mace tear gas attacks both the mucous membrane and the skin to cause a sharp burning sensation that can last more than 30 minutes.

Despite the fact that mace tear gas was not very effective against dogs and other animals and was less effective against drunks, drug abusers, and psychotics it remained popular until the invention of pepper spray. Oleoresin Capsicum (OC) or pepper spray is a derivative of hot cayenne peppers and is an inflammatory chemical agent unlike the irritant agents of tear gas and mace tear gas. Pepper spray inflames breathing tube tissues, dilates eyes for temporary blindness, and burns breathing through the nose and throat. It has the ability to incapacitate dogs, other animals, drunks, drug abusers, psychotics, and everyday criminals. Pepper spray also takes affect almost immediately and since the mucous membrane swells to prevent all but life support breathing it can stop aggressive action for as long as one hour. Flushing the eyes and face with water helps rid the body of the affects of the pepper spray, which does not cause permanent damage.

Above: This officer is wearing a gas mask to protect him from the tear gas. *Photograph courtesy of Leslie O'Shaughnessy Studios*

Left: Pepper spray works at close range with maximum effectiveness depending on the power of the container but it usually is most potent from 2 to 8 feet. *Photograph courtesy of Andrew Gordon*

CHAPTER ONE

Firearms Training

"From 1980 to 1995 there were 13 officers accidentally shot and killed while training." U.S. Department of Justice.

Although shooting a gun is such a small part of a police officer's job, it can also be the most critical part of the job as well. Officers train constantly to prepare themselves for the moment that they will have to shoot someone in protection of themselves or others. Since this is such an important aspect of law enforcement, the training that goes into preparing the officers is crucial.

Shooting at paper targets at the range is one form of training, but for realism some departments have gone to using computer and video simulations to put the officer in a more realistic scenario. Officers interact with training simulations using wireless weapons that are duplicates of their real duty firearms. The officers experience situations where they are required to shoot or not to shoot, seek cover, or are shot at by video suspects. The scenario can then be replayed to show the officer where they shot and what their reaction time was to the simulated threat. As computers become more powerful this technology will continue to

Right: Realistic live-fire training can now be accomplished with simulated ammunition. This ammunition is similar to the paint balls used in paint ball guns but works through service weapons. *Photograph courtesy of Simunition*

Far Right: Video training scenarios allow police officers to interact with a simulated emergency. Instructors can replay how the officer performed in shoot/don't shoot scenarios to help provide more realistic training situations. *Photograph courtesy of FATS, Inc.*

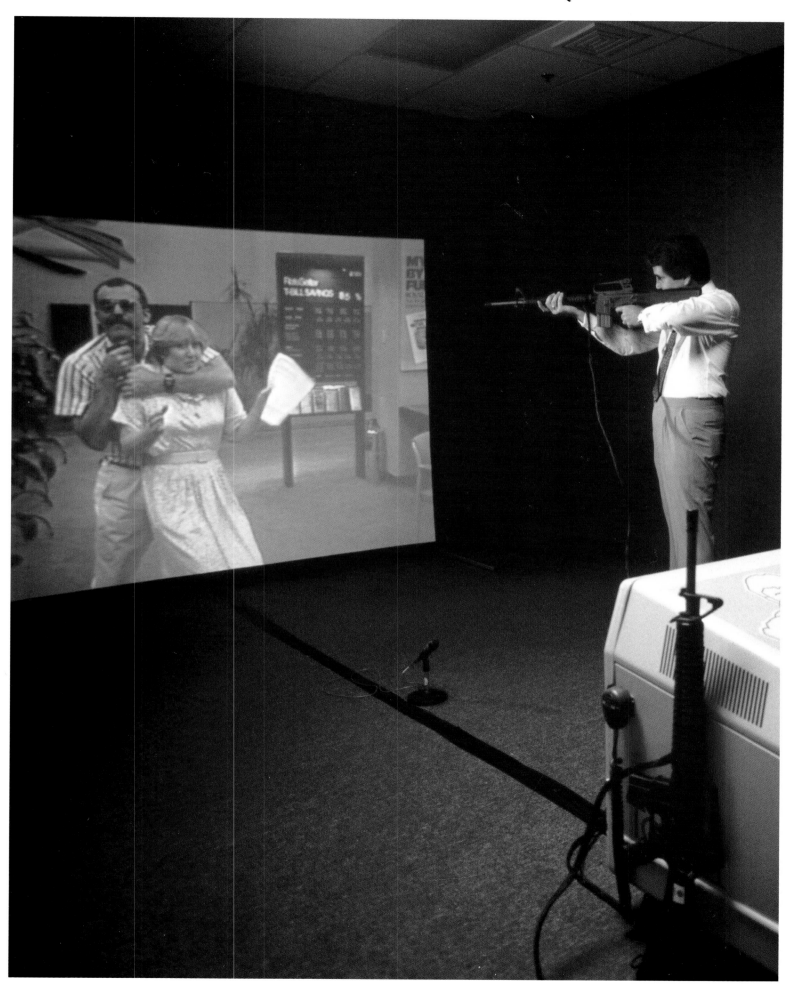

POLICE EQUIPMENT

Above: Another view of the simulated live-fire exercise shows that the officers wear helmets and protective vests to guard sensitive areas of the body.
Photograph courtesy of Simunition

Right: Full contact training with protective padding helps officers deal with the threat of a dangerously aggressive criminal and learn to prevent their service weapon from being taken by the suspect.
Photograph courtesy of Heckler & Koch, Inc.

become a better tool to help law enforcement in training.

Experienced officers in special units like the SWAT team sometimes engage in live-fire exercises. A live-fire exercise consists of officers performing their duties while their weapons are fully loaded and functioning. This type of practice is very dangerous but extremely beneficial. To counter the danger of this exercise, some departments are using ammunition that fires bullets that are made out of a marking substance similar to paint balls instead of real bullets. The officers wear protective clothing as well as helmets that cover the mouth and face and then proceed with the live-fire exercise. When someone is hit they are marked with a small amount of paint much like the recreational paint ball guns. This concept allows officers to have the benefit of training using live ammunition in their weapons yet be completely safe.

CHAPTER TWO
Vehicles

SHERIFF

Left: Helicopters are often used for transporting the critically injured. Here law enforcement officers load an injured comrade into a waiting helicopter. *Photograph courtesy of Heckler & Koch, Inc.*

CHAPTER TWO

Police Cruisers

"In 1914, Berkeley California Police Department was the first law enforcement agency in the country to have all patrol officers using automobiles."

History

Henry Ford made automobiles available and affordable to the common man. By the 1920s, the general public was beginning to travel further and more often then they had previously. The increase in city and town traffic made it necessary to enact traffic laws to promote safety for drivers and pedestrians. It was also necessary for law enforcement to obtain automobiles so that officers could enforce these new laws. Even today,

traffic violations are one of the most recognizable duties of the modern police officer. In 1997, 626,000 people received minor injuries in speeding-related crashes. An additional 75,000 people received moderate injuries and 41,000 received critical injuries in speeding-related crashes (based on methodology from The Economic Cost of Motor Vehicle Crashes 1994, NHTSA).

The automobile changed the way officers policed their beats. Before cruisers, officers

Right: A driver later convicted of D.U.I (driving under the influence) going 60 mph struck this K-9 officer's cruiser from behind at 1:40 p.m. on a sunny Sunday afternoon. The offender's blood alcohol content was 0.17, which is more than twice the legal limit of 0.08. The officer and his K-9 partner were fine. *Photograph courtesy of Randy Mucha*

would walk a neighborhood beat or ride a horse or bicycle, only covering a small area as their beat. With the advent of the cruiser an individual officer could cover a much larger area and have the ability to back up another officer much quicker than before. The cruiser soon became one of the most important tools in modern law enforcement, along with the gun and the two-way radio. The cruiser became the police officer's office; keeping the officer dry when writing a police report, holding personal gear in addition to other emergency equipment that the officer may need while on duty. In addition, the cruiser could be used for a single officer to transport multiple criminals to jail as well as enable the officer to arrive at the crime scene faster than on foot, horseback, or bicycle.

Prior to 1910 very few people owned an automobile and most roads were not paved and did not provide a reliable surface for automobile travel. By 1920, more of the general public was able to buy an automobile and paved highways were built to accommodate the increased traffic, making automobile traveling cheaper and easier. American society gained more mobility when the automobile gave them the freedom to travel all over the country. The automobile made most mounted police officers switch to the car as well as non-motorized bicycle officers migrate to driving a cruiser.

Criminals also gained the mobility that came with the automobile and used it to their advantage. They began to rob banks and commit crimes in one area and then drive a greater distance to their hideout. Local police departments that did not have the use of the automobile, two-way radio (which had yet to be invented), or centralized police departments (like a state police or strong federal agency) were nearly powerless to catch these criminals. Since the police departments of that time did not yet have the national databanks of information or most of the other tools modern law enforcement has today, they created State police departments. The State police departments' main objective was to respond to the change in criminal behavior (increased mobility) and help patrol the new highways.

Crime waves spurred on by the popularity of the automobile were taking their toll on American society. From 1932 to 1934,

"Bonnie and Clyde" and their gang (a notorious group of outlaw bank robbers) murdered more than ten law enforcement officers while committing robberies in a crime wave. Local police departments did not have the equipment or resources to control the criminal activity or the unlawful gangs of the day since the gangs would often travel across state lines to hideouts in another police jurisdiction. Due to the increase in criminals crossing state lines to escape law enforcement, the federal government decided to create a national law enforcement unit to protect the welfare of the general public. Under J. Edgar Hoover, the Federal Bureau of Investigation (FBI) staked their claim as the nations premier law enforcement agency. The FBI created task forces to arrest the Dellingers and the "Bonnie and Clydes" of the day and put an end to the invincibility of the automobile driven gangs and their multi-state rampages.

Above: Police are video taping more of their activities since the cost of video equipment has come down and the power of video taped evidence helps juries see what the officer sees. Often video tape evidence will forestall days of expensive and time consuming testimony.
Photograph courtesy of Leslie O'Shaughnessy Studios

Right: This is a good shot of a standard police uniform with cap and tie. Although the tie looks professional it is of the clip-on variety so that a suspect can not use it as a weapon against the officer. *Photograph courtesy of Leslie O'Shaughnessy Studios*

The Patrol Car

Only certain types of automobiles can be used as good, everyday patrol cars (more commonly known as cruisers, but also called the scout car). Of course, there are a variety of specialty cruisers made out of sports cars, station wagons, and sport utility vehicles but for the most part the car of choice is a boxy, four door, mid-size automobile with lots of horsepower. The reason for using a mid-sized car is because the cruiser is the "office" for the officer who will spend many hours on patrol in it and will have to transport at least two prisoners so the back seat has to be large. The reason for using a car with lots of horsepower is because the cruiser requires a big V-8 engine to be able to respond to an emergency situation quickly as well as to keep-up in high-speed vehicle pursuits.

Members of the general public who are interested in law enforcement equipment and practices often believe that police cruisers receive a "police package" of automobile upgrades from the vehicle manufacturer. These mythical special options are supposed to allow the cruiser to do much more than the standard automobile available to the public. In reality, the cruiser is built with more options than the standard car but not enough to make it too different. The typical "police package" consists of a heavy-duty frame and cross members, increased suspension and upgraded brakes, calibrated speedometers. In addition, the air conditioning is automatically switched off at high speed to save on power being drained from the engine when it's needed most along with dual fans to keep the engine cool.

Cruisers come predrilled from the manufacturer for the emergency lights that go on top and next to the grill. The paint scheme and logo on the sides of the cruiser are completely up to the jurisdiction but usually "police," "sheriff," or "state police" is clearly inscribed in a prominent place. In the well between the driver and front-passenger seat all of the police emergency activation equipment is loaded. The emergency activation equipment has switches for the lights, hood lights (commonly called takedown lights), and side alley lights. There are several siren switches for the different alarm sounds so that each officer responding to an emergency can choose a different alarm sound from the other cruisers responding to the same emergency to alert people to the more than one cruiser. Also included in the emergency activation equipment is a

Left: In traffic situations, the standard police uniform includes a reflective vest. This is something that police take seriously because nearly 800 officers died in the line of duty since 1980 as a result of traffic accidents. *Photograph courtesy of Leslie O'Shaughnessy Studios*

Right: Often the entire backseat of a cruiser is replaced with a solid plastic seat. This is because a hastily searched suspect will try to dump their drugs or weapons before they get to jail and have a thorough search conducted. Plus, some suspects will bleed, urinate, or defecate in the backseat and in these cases the plastic makes it easier to keep hygienic.

Far Right: The power of the computer allows officers to conduct checks for stolen vehicles, wanted persons, the writing of reports, and many other things from the comfort of their own cruiser. *Photograph courtesy Electronic Systems Technology, Inc.*

two-way radio with battery charger and a microphone for an intercom system.

In the case of the cruisers rear seats where prisoners will be placed for transportation, the car is changed quite drastically. First, the door handles and window controls are taken out so that criminals will not be able to escape. Even the door locks are rerouted so they are controlled by the driver's (the officer) position. Next, a solid panel is placed in between the front seats and rear seats of the car to separate and protect the driver from the prisoners in the back. Usually there is a plexiglass sliding window installed so that only the officer can open it to speak to the prisoner and close it if the prisoner is abusive or spitting. In a lot of the cruisers the rear seat is taken out and a one-piece plastic seat is inserted. The solid plastic seat prevents prisoners from unloading drugs or weapons without being detected and makes the cruiser easier to clean if the prisoner urinates, defecates, or bleeds in the rear seat. The officer can simply hose the rear seat down to keep it hygienic.

Modern Police and the Automobile

The drawback to using cruisers for policing was that officers became removed from the citizens they protected and served. Complaints began to surface from people that felt they no longer knew the officer that worked in their neighborhood like they did when police walked a beat. So more than fifty years after the automobile revolutionized police departments, police departments realized that everyday officer-to-citizen contact with its citizens was a significant asset and have begun to make changes in the way they patrol the streets. Many police departments have gone back to community policing and now encourage officers to live and work in a specific neighborhood. The vast majority of officers still patrol their beats using the cruiser but the modern officer now gets to emergency situations using an assortment of transportation like the motorcycle, mountain bike, horse, snowmobile, all-terrain-vehicle, helicopter, plane, boat, and just about anything else that will take them.

Right: Here is the driver-side view of a felony vehicle stop. This type of vehicle stop is conducted for officer safety. The occupant is considered too dangerous to approach normally so officers will use as much of the vehicle as possible to shield their bodies while ordering the driver to come to them.

Far Right, Top: This cruiser is outfitted with a push-bar on the front bumper. This is used to help push stranded automobiles out of mud and snow. It can also ram the bumper of fleeing vehicles to knock them off the road and end dangerous pursuits.

Right: The two officers involved in this felony vehicle stop will work together to help bring this dangerous situation to a close without the loss of life. One of the first priorities is to get the car turned off and the suspects hands out in the open where the officers can see them.

Far Right, Below: Although cruisers are generally the same boxy four doors throughout the country, each jurisdiction can put almost any logo or color pattern they want to decorate the exterior.

Right: This nighttime photograph shows all the emergency lights that a police car needs to respond to an emergency safely. *Photograph courtesy of Whelen Engineering Company, Inc.*

Below: The V-8 engine has been the engine of choice with officers for a long time. The power and quick acceleration gets the officers to the emergency the quickest. *Photograph courtesy Whelen Engineering Company, Inc.*

Above: Traffic stops are very dangerous even when the officer is simply helping a motorist, so vehicle position and emergency lights are key for officer safety. *Photograph courtesy of Whelen Engineering Company, Inc.*

CHAPTER TWO

Motorcycles

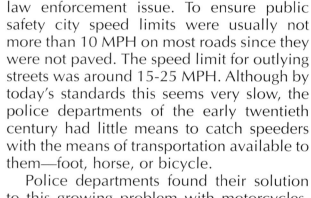

Below: Here is a view of the motorcycle officer's controls for the radio, loudspeaker, radar gun, siren/police lights, as well as the switches and gears for the motorcycle itself. *Photograph courtesy of Squad-Fitter's, Inc.*

In 1905, many of the larger police departments started to use the motorcycle as a way to increase the efficiency of their service to the public. Prior to the introduction of the motorcycle, most police departments could not afford an automobile, and even if they could afford an automobile, the automobiles were not as practical as an officer on foot, horseback, or bicycle patrol.

With the surge of automobile ownership during this time, speeding, reckless driving and automobile accidents became a major

law enforcement issue. To ensure public safety city speed limits were usually not more than 10 MPH on most roads since they were not paved. The speed limit for outlying streets was around 15-25 MPH. Although by today's standards this seems very slow, the police departments of the early twentieth century had little means to catch speeders with the means of transportation available to them—foot, horse, or bicycle.

Police departments found their solution to this growing problem with motorcycles. Motorcycles of this era reached speeds of 50 MPH and were much more affordable than automobiles. When the speedometer was invented around this same time, the motorcycle officer was able to catch speeders and prove in a court of law how fast the speeder was going so that they could be legally reprimanded to curb the threat to the public.

Although the automobile is the most used mode of transportation for the modern police department the motorcycle still provides great service with it's increased agility, high visibility, and accessibility to the public. The police motorcycle can move through heavy traffic much more easily than a cruiser. With its quick acceleration and ability to stay out of view, the motorcycle is ideal for apprehending speeding violators. Overall, the police motorcycle provides the ideal solution for enforcing traffic laws, providing police escorts, and controlling traffic flow.

Typically, police motorcycle units are the experts in traffic law and enforcement for their jurisdictions. Police motorcycle units usually are experienced accident investigators and are well trained in the specialized

Left: On the back of this motorcycle we can see the panniers carrying the officers gear, emergency equipment, and paperwork. *Photograph courtesy of Leslie O'Shaughnessy Studios*

skills needed to provide escort for dignitaries, funerals, and heavy equipment.

An officer does not have to have extensive motorcycle riding experience or even know how to ride a motorcycle to be a motor officer. The only requirement for the officer is to exhibit the ability and desire to be trained for this duty. Training usually lasts more than eight weeks and is both physically and mentally demanding. The typical police motorcycle is often large and normally weighs over 750lbs. The officer must learn to successfully operate the machine in extremely slow and fast speeds and avoid multiple hazards while operating the bike in a safe manner.

Since the motorcycle's introduction to the equipment of the police department, it has always enjoyed a unique status among officers. It is extremely visible in ceremonial events, extremely effective in law enforcement action, and extremely beneficial to the police department as a whole.

Above: For high-risk situations the motorcycle officer is trained to use the bike as protection from the threat. Here the officer crouches in a modified Weaver stance (a two handed pistol stance) behind his motorcycle. *Photograph courtesy of Squad-Fitter's, Inc.*

Right: Another view of a high-risk stop, one can see that the motorcycle officer has taken proper cover and is in a better position to direct the movements of the driver. Here the officer has ordered the driver to put his hands out of the window so he can see them. *Photograph courtesy of Squad-Fitter's, Inc.*

Left: The motorcycle is perfect for traffic enforcement duties because of its acceleration and maneuverability. *Photograph courtesy of Leslie O'Shaughnessy Studios*

Above: Many police departments have super-highways that a motorcycle built for speed can be very useful on.
Photograph courtesy of Squad-Fitter's, Inc.

Right: On the other hand, many police departments have back country or wooded areas that the cruiser can not reach so the dirt bike comes in handy for these situations.
Photograph courtesy of Squad-Fitter's, Inc.

Right: This officer is using a radar gun to monitor the speed of passing vehicles. The radar gun emits radar waves that reflect off of the moving vehicle and back to the radar gun, the machine then reads the change in frequency (the Doppler effect) of the waves to determine the speed.
Photograph courtesy of Leslie O'Shaughnessy Studios

Below: The panniers fill up quickly for the motorcycle officer so the radar gun gets its own holster. The readily accessible holster allows the officer to chase after speeding motorists.

Left: Motorcycle training is an intense course where officers learn to master the bike at extremely slow and high speeds. Here an officer maneuvers the motorcycle through a tight circle of cones. *Photograph courtesy of Leslie O'Shaughnessy Studios*

Left: Here is an excellent shot of a motorcycle with sidecar. *Photograph courtesy of Squad-Fitter's, Inc.*

Above: Motorcycle officers earn the right to wear an additional patch of a winged wheel that denotes their status in this special unit.

Right: Motorcycle officers perform special duties and assignments. Here they are escorting foreign dignitaries. The maneuverability and visibility the motorcycle provides is important in these situations. *Photograph courtesy of the San Francisco Police Department*

CHAPTER TWO

Air Unit

In the 1960s the U.S. military was using helicopters to rescue wounded, deliver troops to the field, and perform reconnaissance functions in the Vietnam War. Pilots who came home from the war to become police officers extolled the virtues of the helicopter and the civilian benefits. Soon helicopters were being used throughout the country to shuttle accident victims to hospitals and provide eyes in the sky for police on the ground.

With a top speed around 140 mph the helicopter provided an excellent addition to the vehicle pursuit. Fleeing suspects can try to elude the officers on the ground but rarely can they outrun a helicopter hovering above them.

Additional equipment was added to the helicopter like stabilized binoculars, spotlights and infrared systems. The stabilized binoculars allow officers to read a moving license plate from nearly 300 feet. The spotlights provide instant daylight for ground officers searching for suspects. The infrared systems allow the helicopter officer to "see" people through cover by the detection of body heat.

Right: In the bottom front of this State Trooper helicopter you can clearly see the remote controlled high-powered light, with an infrared imaging system right behind it. This helicopter is also used in medical evacuation as seen by the medical marker on the rear fin. *Photo courtesy of Bell Helicopter Textron*

Left: The helicopter pilot can direct the police on the ground and vice versa even when there are multiple police jurisdictions involved using the radio and dispatchers.
Photo courtesy of Bell Helicopter Textron

Left: A three-quarter view of the helicopter wearing the familiar NYPD livery sitting on the trolley used to maneuver it in and out of the hangar.

CHAPTER TWO

Bicycle Equipment

Below: The mountain bike has allowed the police officer to be more approachable to the public and thus more effective as a tool for fighting crime.
Photograph courtesy of Olympic Uniforms, J. Marcel Enterprises

The first time that bicycles were used in law enforcement was in the 1880s. Bicycles were the newest mode of transportation in the nation and proved to be a huge benefit to law enforcement. Police departments were searching for a better way to patrol their beats other than walking or riding a horse and automobiles were not yet available due to prohibitive costs. Since the bicycle was inexpensive, easy to maneuver, and reliable, it was able to meet the police need. For 20 years police used bicycles to patrol the street.

It was not until the invention of the motorcycle and the availability of affordable automobiles that the bicycle was mostly retired from police service. The new cruiser was not slowed down by weather, posed no physical restrictions to the officer driving it, and enabled officers to transport passengers and criminals. Although the migration from the bicycle to the faster moving cruisers and motorcycles appeared to be a very positive enhancement, the police lost an avenue of valuable personal communication with the public.

The general public was apprehensive about approaching police when the officers were in their cruisers. Driving a cruiser did not allow officers to easily stop, get out of the cruiser, and to get to know the people on their beat. When people saw officers get out of the cruiser, they assumed it was only to apprehend a criminal. People began to complain that they did not know the officers who patrolled their neighborhood. They wanted local law enforcement to return to the day when an officer walked a neighborhood beat, knew the people that lived there, and was a more integral part of the neighborhood. They wanted a more identifiable role model for their children, someone to assist them on resolving civil issues, and someone to answer their questions about the law and how it pertained to them.

So, one-hundred years later after the first bicycle was introduced to a police department, in the late 1980s, the bicycle was re-introduced to police departments. This time it came in the form of a sporty mountain bike with a sturdier frame and thick, all-terrain tires. As soon as police officers started using the new mountain bike for patrol in limited numbers, they began to discover what an advantage a bicycle had in giving the general public a positive view of police.

Left: Training usually lasts for a week or more for bicycle officers. *Photograph courtesy of the International Police Mountain Bike Association*

Above: This photograph shows the equipment of a typical bicycle officer. Note the panniers (saddlebags) that hold emergency equipment and paper work. The microphone hanging on her chest is the extension for the radio and she is wearing her helmet.

Above Right: Bicycle officers train on all obstacles they will encounter in their normal duties. *Photograph courtesy of the International Police Mountain Bike Association*

Far Right: Officers train for obstacles that are not encountered everyday. Training for the unforeseen is key to overcoming barriers in emergency situations. *Photograph courtesy of the International Police Mountain Bike Association*

No longer were officers deemed unapproachable and non-caring, now the new bicycle officers bridged the gap between the foot officer and officers in the cruisers. The public responded to the bicycle officers with enthusiasm and approached officers on the mountain bike more often than those in cruisers. Another advantage to adding bicycles as police transportation was that officers began to host bicycle safety courses for the neighborhoods they patrolled, opening up another outlet to regain the relationship that officers once had with the citizens on their neighborhood beats.

The only citizens not to embrace the modern bicycle are criminals. Using their mountain bikes officers are able to go in places the cruiser can not due to their size and the noise that they make. Because the

Far Right: Even the Military Police (MP) have gotten on the mountain bike craze. Here you see the different uniforms of the Military Police as they patrol vast military reservations in the U.S. and abroad. *Photograph courtesy of the International Police Mountain Bike Association*

Right: Bicycle officers need to know how to defend themselves since the bicycle can quickly and silently bring the officer upon criminal activity. Here an officer trains how to strike someone with her baton while simultaneously guarding her sidearm from being taken by the suspect in the struggle. *Photograph courtesy of the RRB Systems International*

Below Right: Officers learn to throw their mountain bikes down on the ground when emergencies arise. Officer safety is the primary concern and the wear and tear on the bicycle comes last. *Photograph courtesy of the International Police Mountain Bike Association*

bicycle makes little sound the officers can hear more allowing them to respond quicker and quieter to the situation. The mountain bike has been dubbed the "stealth" vehicle because officers have been known to ride right up on crimes in progress without being detected by the criminals.

Police departments have no problem recruiting officers for this assignment. Bicycle officers readily volunteer for this position and generally go through a week of training to learn the skills that they need to be effective in patrolling an area. Mountain bike training involves advanced riding skills,

obstacle courses like curbs and slalom, emergency stopping, and defensive tactics.

Typical police bicycle equipment is not uncommon for someone who is an avid bicycle rider. The mountain bikes have dual headlights with rechargeable batteries for night patrolling, a water bottle to reduce the risk of dehydration to the officer, and a bike stand. However, there are other police equipment options that most people do not have like a rear rack with panniers (saddle bags to hold paper work and emergency equipment) and police logos or placards signaling that the bicycle is a police vehicle.

CHAPTER TWO

Marine Unit

Below: Sheriff's Deputies conduct the investigation of an air show accident of a single engine plane that crashed into the lake killing the pilot. *Photo courtesy of John and Barb Schertzer*

Law enforcement agencies with significant bodies of water in their jurisdiction will have a marine unit that coordinates the many events involving the municipality's waterway. Marine units provide traffic control and water safety coverage for everyday operation in addition to special events like boat parades and air & sea shows. The marine unit is in charge of all investigations on the water, search and rescue, and dignitary protection. Simple enforcement of the lifejacket laws keep officers busy since the U. S. Coast Guard estimates that of the 500 people who drowned in 1996, 440 of them were not wearing a lifejacket. Law enforcement officers are kept busy especially with the thousands of recreational boaters on the water.

Above: Police use small boats to control, search, and enforce laws on lakes, rivers, and ports nationwide. *Photograph courtesy of Leslie O'Shaughnessy Studios*

Left: Law enforcement divers use boats of all sizes to accomplish their missions. Here an officer gets ready to board a small craft to search for evidence under the bridge (seen in the background). *Photograph courtesy of Leslie O'Shaughnessy Studios*

CHAPTER TWO

Other Police Vehicles

Some law enforcement vehicles are used by just a few departments and thus are unique. These vehicles come into use either because the jurisdiction has a particular type of geography or the department is trying something new. Nevertheless, here are some vehicles that might not be found in your hometown.

The law enforcement community makes use of almost all vehicles to help in keeping the streets safe for the public. The different vehicles range from bicycles to snowmo-

Right: Police utilize the mobility and speed of snowmobiles in snow covered regions to improve their ability to carry out their duties year round. Note the snowshoes the officer is carrying to walk in deep snow.
Photograph courtesy of Leslie O'Shaughnessy Studios

Left: Officers take training courses to learn how to use each piece of equipment they are assigned to operate. *Photograph courtesy of Heckler & Koch, Inc.*

POLICE EQUIPMENT

biles, motorbikes to vans, and armored personnel carriers to helicopters. Some departments, like New York City Police Department, are large enough that their fleet of vehicles may just be all types. The next several pages show a sampling of just how many different types of vehicles they have.

In very dangerous situations the Emergency Services Unit is called out and they have to be ready for any situation. Their heavy duty truck carries a lot of gear from the "Jaws of Life" to scuba equipment.

Three-wheeled motorcycles are not a common site on the road but this one does provide more stability for the officer plus added storage room in the back for emergency equipment.
Photograph courtesy of Squad-Fitters, Inc.

Left: These SWAT officers use an armored car for cover and concealment as they move to a better tactical position.
Photograph courtesy of Heckler & Koch, Inc.

Left (main picture): SWAT team members leap into action off of an armored truck. These types of trucks are commonly used to transport money from stores to banks. But, since these trucks are heavily armored, this department has outfitted it with emergency lights and equipment for SWAT duty.
Photograph courtesy of 21 st Century Hard Armor Protection, Inc.

Far Left: SWAT officers quickly deploy out of the back of a modified armored vehicle.
Photograph courtesy of Heckler & Koch, Inc.

The vehicles on the following pages all belong to the New York City Police Department, showing the diversity of vehicles operated.

Above: In very dangerous situations the Emergency Services Unit is called out. This heavy duty truck carries a lot of their gear from the "Jaws of Life" to scuba equipment.

Right: Here is the NYPD air sea rescue helicopter with the winch and rescue basket hanging out of the open side door. It sits on the trolley so it can be easily maneuvered in and out of the hanger.

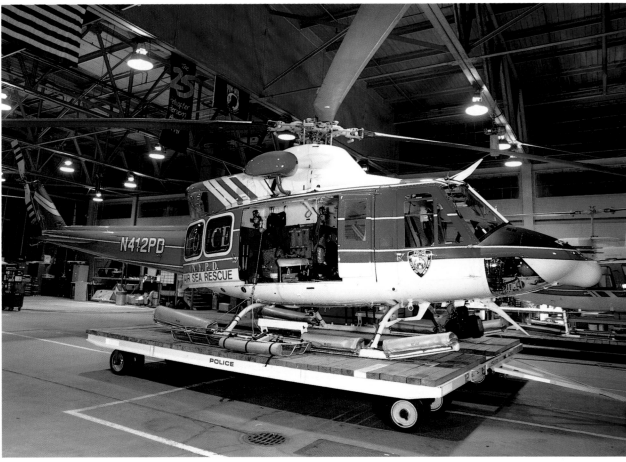

Left, Top, Middle, and Bottom: Every jurisdiction has the authority to paint the exterior of the cruiser with any pattern or logo they want or even all different patterns. Here are three separate versions. Note that the light blue cruiser has the car number 1681 on the trunk of the cruiser as well as on the side; this is to let helicopter units communicate with the ground units.

Right: NYPD uses the standard horse trailer to transport the horse and rider to the various parts of the city that they will patrol.

Below: This armored personnel carrier looks very military but provides a great service to officers when they must face snipers, bombs, and all other sorts of dangerous suspects.

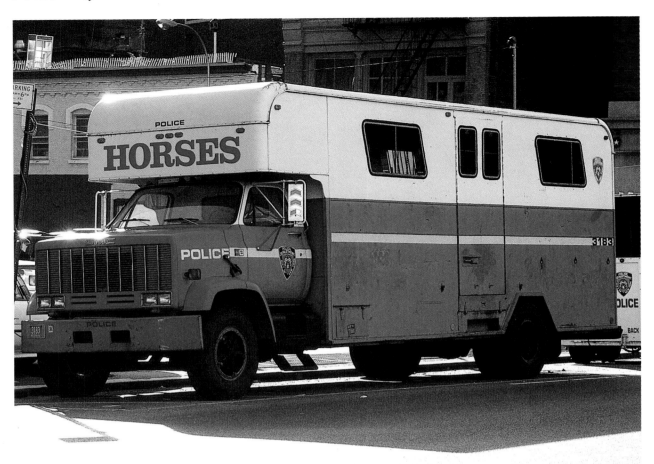

Left: The three-wheeled scooter does not conjure up the "macho" image of a V-8 engine cruiser but it does allow the officer to go where a car cannot while keeping the officer protected from the elements.

Below: The station wagon can haul more equipment than a regular cruiser, yet still provide some of the same patrol ability. The bomb squad is using this wagon but identification technicians and other special assignment units also use it.

Right, Top and Middle: Here are two views of this heavy truck used by the Emergency Services Unit. Notice the enormous front bumper that is reinforced to allow the truck to push large objects out of its path.

Right: The police van is a versatile vehicle that allows the department to either carry multiple prisoners or lots of equipment.

CHAPTER THREE
Other Equipment

CHAPTER THREE

Patrol Officer Duty Equipment

Right and Middle Right: Expandable batons are for regular patrol use but detectives and "plain clothes" officers like them since they can fit into pockets easily.

Bottom Right: Side-handle batons allow the officer to defend as well as strike.

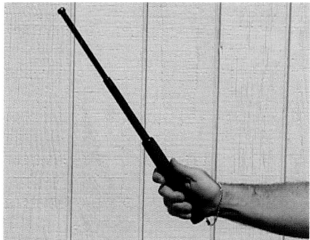

This section will cover the general equipment that a regular patrol officer typically carries on their beat. The modern officer carries quite a lot of equipment from batons to handcuffs, bullet resistant vests to radios. This total weight of all of these pieces of equipment can add up to an extra 10 to 15 lbs. that officers may carry with them everywhere on their beat. However, all of this gear is necessary in one capacity or another for the officer to successfully serve the public and protect themself.

The Baton

Early law enforcement officers carried nothing more than a glorified club. It was a wooden stick with a rope through it so the officer could carry it more easily. In the early 20th century some officers began carrying a slap-jack which was a leather strap with lead inserted in one end. The slap-jack was small and could be carried in the back pocket. The leaded end when handled correctly could deliver a heavy whack to a violent suspect. The slap-jack has lost favor with police departments, and although it is still carried by a few officers it is virtually obsolete.

Straight wood batons were the intermediate less-than-lethal option for police for many years until the early 1970s when the side-handle baton was introduced. Even today, the traditional baton is authorized for use by just more than half of all police departments. The ability to make a baton with a sturdy side handle started with the invention of thermoplastics.

The side-handle baton quickly became a favorite with police departments. This new

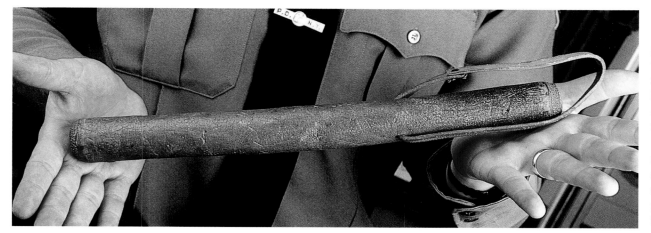

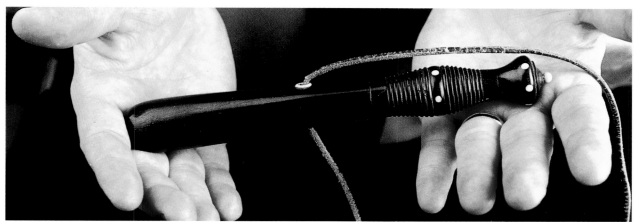

Left: Although this rough branch, complete with leather thong, is called a nightstick, it is really little more than a club. This one was used in the 1800s.

Middle Left: This shows a pearl-studded daystick used by police at the turn-of-the-century.

Bottom Left: This is an excellent photo of modern wooden straight batons.

type of baton provided officers with multiple options for gaining and maintaining control of a non-compliant suspect. The side handle allowed the officer to spin the baton in his hand to deliver a blow, punch with the short or long end when grabbed by the handle, and perform blocks. When maneuvered deftly, the baton can be used to maintain control of a suspect through arm bars and pain compliance. Another baton just coming onto the police market is a sort of hybrid of the straight and side-handle batons. This baton seems to allow the officer to rotate from defensive positions to offensive positions quicker than the side-handle baton.

Expandable versions of both the straight and the side-handle baton were also invented. These expandable versions allowed the officer to carry a small pocket sized baton on their police belt, and when needed, flick the baton to its fully functioning size. The batons use either the friction lock or a positive lock to stay expanded.

Extensive training is needed for an officer to be skilled enough to use the baton to its full capacity. Officers must learn where to strike a violent suspect to minimize the possibility of injury or death while ensuring their own safety.

Right: This bicycle officer is using the baton to strike the suspect to her rear, which is one of the many strike positions of the baton. *Photograph courtesy of RRB Systems International*

Right: An officer demonstrates a new baton design in a protective stance. *Photograph courtesy of RRB Systems International*

Left: This officer wields his baton to stop an enraged, but unarmed attacker. Notice that the officer is looking to hit the suspect in the shins which is a non-life threatening but potentially painful strike.
Photograph courtesy of RRB Systems International

Right: Here are four old-style handcuffs that show the evolution of cuffs from the original manacles (near right) to contemporary styles pictures on the right side. Notice the standardized key with a red ribbon attached in the bottom picture.

Handcuffs

Early manacles were crude pieces of equipment that a blacksmith would have to attach. A heavy ball and chain would be attached to prevent prisoners from escaping. Prisoners would have to pick up this ball and carry it or drag it along while they walked. Metalworking technology allowed future law enforcement officers to have machine made metal handcuffs that were all identical with interchangeable parts. Making all handcuffs identical allowed the manufacturers to adopt a standard for a key to unlock all brands of handcuffs. Modern day officers use many different brands of handcuffs while using only one key.

Disposable restraining devices designed to be used only once are also used by police departments throughout the country. These restraining devices are made out of flexible plastic and can supplement the officer's regular handcuffs. The plastic cuff can be drawn tight around feet, hands or linked to each other in order to hinder escape. They are very useful in mass arrest situations like demonstrations where police need to place many people under arrest in a short period of time. Unruly suspects that kick violently can have plastic cuffs put around ankles to provide protection to the officer, property, and themselves. Although these plastic cuffs are useful they will only complement, but never replace, existing metal handcuffs because plastic is so much easier to defeat than metal.

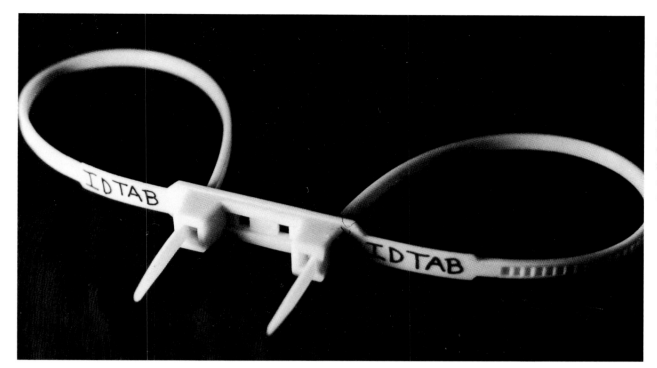

Left: Plastic cuffs are generally used when officers are going to make mass arrests due to unruly demonstrations, riots, or sting operations and need to quickly detain and transport suspects. *Photograph courtesy of Tuff-Cuff*

Left: This arrest represents a typical arrest scenario. The officer uses the car as a support for the suspect, then stands safely behind the suspect in order to handcuff and search him. *Photograph courtesy of Leslie O'Shaughnessy*

Right: This officer is using the prone position, a safer position for searching and detaining potentially violent suspects. *Photograph courtesy of Leslie O'Shaughnessy Studios*

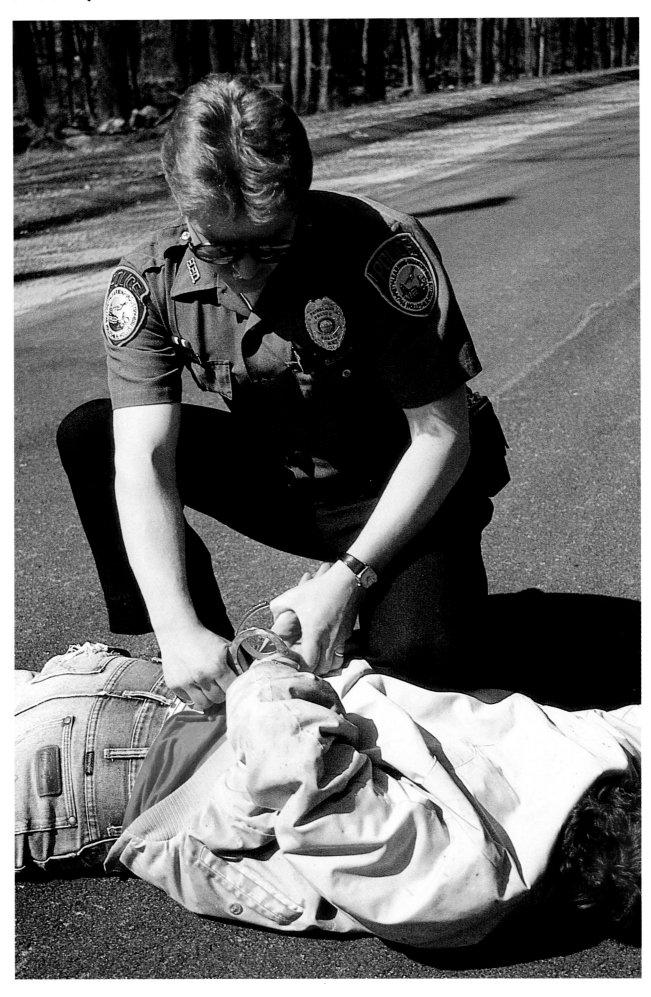

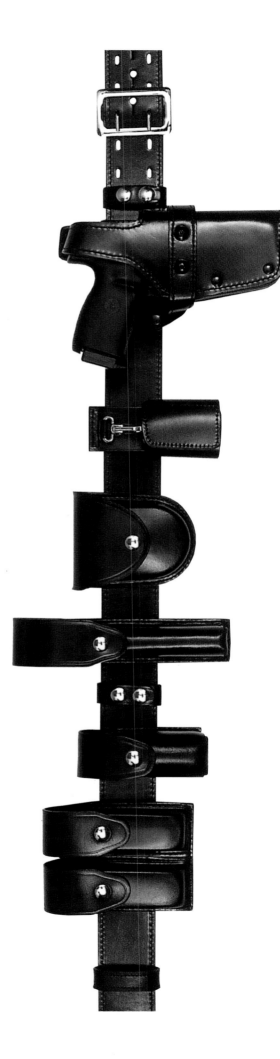

Police Belt

The police belt, often called the "Sam Browne" belt, is made of leather or vinyl and holds all of the patrol officer's duty gear. Officers position the equipment on the belt according to their needs. For example, left-handed officers put the service handgun on the left side. The belt carries their handgun, extra ammunition magazines for their handgun, handcuffs, pepper spray, radio, baton, flashlight, keys, latex gloves holder, and whatever else an officer feels they might need for patrol duties.

Far Left: Here is a typical leather belt set-up for patrol officers. It holds all of the necessary items like a handgun, extra magazine pouches for ammunition, handcuff case, flashlight, baton, pepper spray, car keys holder, and room for extra items like latex gloves for searches.
Photograph courtesy of Gould & Goodrich

Near Left, Top to Bottom: Officers have the ability to choose exactly how they want to wear their patrol equipment. Officers will position items according to comfort and ease of movement so that in a crisis they will know exactly where to go for each item.

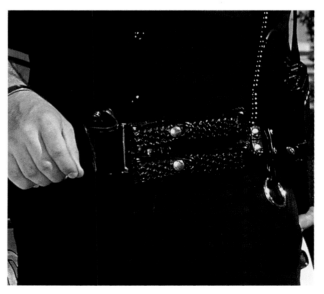

CHAPTER THREE

Body Armor & Protective Clothing

Thousands of years ago when people fought with swords, spears, and arrows they defended themselves with shields, helmets, and body armor. Until the invention of gunpowder, people wore as much protection as they could from the devastating affects of the weapons of the day. When gunpowder was invented it allowed the bullet to pass through all metal armor making the shield, helmet, and breastplate useless for protec-

Right: The lead SWAT team officer holds the ballistic shield up to protect the body yet keeps an eye out for the suspect as he advances toward the scene.
Photograph courtesy of 21st Century Hard Armor Protection, Inc.

tion. The Battle of Bicocca in 1522 proved that firearms would be the weapons of the future when the metal armor was ineffective against gunpowder propelled projectiles. For hundreds of years, wars were fought without any bullet/shrapnel protection at all (our revolutionary war all the way up to World War I). It was not until World War I that soldiers started wearing helmets again for protection against deadly shrapnel caused by artillery.

However, people had not given up on body armor. Thick silk shirts were worn by important people of the day and police experimented wearing hard metal sheets in the early 20th century but nothing worked consistently. By the time of World War II and the Korean War, the U.S. military was wearing versions of body armor with limited success. It was not until the late 1960s and early 1970s that protective ballistic materials were designed that were light enough to be worn and yet strong enough to stop most forms of small caliber bullets. Modern day body armor does not make someone "Superman" with bullets simply ricocheting off ones chest. The impact of a bullet is felt like a sledgehammer and often causes severe bruising.

In 1974, police officers started using soft body armor. The protective ballistic materials were at first woven together in several layers, but now ballistic material innovations are incorporating non-woven fibers into body armor design. Soft body armor operates by catching a bullet in a net-like web of very strong fibers. The difference between soft and hard body armor is that soft armor is designed to stop small arms

Left: This officer uses his clear riot shield to restrain a suspect from furthering his aggressive behavior. *Photograph courtesy of 21st Century Hard Armor Protection, Inc.*

Below: SWAT teams need the extra body armor because the situations they routinely handle are more dangerous, especially rapid entry deployments like this one. *Photograph courtesy of Heckler & Koch, Inc.*

"On average, more than 65,000 law enforcement officers are assaulted each year and some 3,000 are injured annually. A total of 1,624 law enforcement officers died in the line of duty during the last 10 years, an average of one death every 54 hours or 162 per year. Of the 60 or so officers that are annually shot to death, it is estimated that wearing body armor saves an additional 20."

ammunition and to be worn in a concealed manner. Hard armor (tactical armor) is usually donned over soft armor and is designed to stop rifle fire (SWAT teams usually wear this tactical armor).

Body armor is designed to offer protection from ballistic threats under specific circumstances. This means that body armor is not "bullet-proof," nor will it make a person immune to all threats. Body armor is designed for various uses, for instance a patrol officer will wear light weight soft body armor which gives the most maneuverability but the least protection. Bomb technicians will wear up to 45lbs. of body armor that allow for the least amount of maneuverability but the most protection. Correctional officers that face a much greater threat from knives or shives wear non-ballistic protective vests that are puncture resistant for protection.

Protective shields for SWAT teams and riot shields for crowd control provide a measure of portable protection. Some SWAT ballistic shields are heavier and need to be wheeled into action. However, the heavy design has the ability to protect the officer from high-powered rifle fire yet still provide a full view of the threat. The riot shield is meant to be a lightweight defense against thrown objects with some versions of the shield able to withstand handgun rounds.

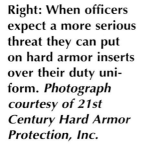

Right: When officers expect a more serious threat they can put on hard armor inserts over their duty uniform. *Photograph courtesy of 21st Century Hard Armor Protection, Inc.*

Left: Today, most Police Officers wear a bullet resistant vest under there uniform. These vests are made of layers of interwoven bullet-resistant material that can stop most small caliber bullets. *Photograph courtesy of Leslie O'Shaughnessy Studios*

CHAPTER THREE

SWAT Equipment

Many law enforcement agencies have formed Special Weapons and Tactics units (SWAT) or at least have access to them. SWAT teams go by other names such as Emergency Response Team, Special Response Team, Quick Response Team, Special Operations Team, or Special Enforcement Unit but they all have a similar mission. The mission of the SWAT team is to respond to critical incidents, perform high-risk warrant service, and deal with most of the other extremely hazardous law enforcement assignments.

Highly trained police units that specialize in resolving critical incidents started in the mid 1960s as criminals began to arm themselves better, street gangs became bigger and more violent, and the number of extremists and hate groups increased. Tragic events were taking place throughout America and the World that the typical patrol officer was ill equipped to handle. For instance, in 1966 a man armed with a high-powered rifle climbed up to the University of Texas Clock Tower Building in Austin and killed over a dozen people and wounded more than thirty because the police could not get near the suspect to stop him.

The Texas Tower Sniper as it has come to be remembered best shows the reason why SWAT units were created. The sniper was well armed, he had 3 rifles, 2 handguns, a saw-off shotgun, hundreds of rounds of ammunition, and a can of gasoline. The sniper had climbed a tower over 300 feet tall which overlooked a large part of the

Right: Sometimes the element of surprise is best. These SWAT officers are preparing to climb down from the roof. They are wearing balaclavas over their faces to protect their skin from injury and in some undercover situations, prevent suspects from identifying them.
Photograph courtesy of Leslie O'Shaughnessy Studios

campus. The sniper shot a pregnant woman, medics who came to the scene, and people that looked out of their windows to see what was happening. The police that were called to the scene did not know what to do. These types of crimes had rarely happened before and there were no plans of action and no unit to respond to such a crisis. The police could not get close enough to the tower to stop the sniper nor could they help the wounded. A police plane that flew over head backed away when it came under fire as well. In the end, the police found an underground tunnel that led to the tower and in a shoot-out they killed the sniper but not until there were so many innocent people killed and wounded first.

These types of incidents alerted police chiefs across the country to the changing face of crime and the need for a specialized unit that could handle all kinds of emergencies. SWAT teams were formed and equipped to carry out this new mission. Since the inception of the SWAT team, the missions they are called to handle have increased to constantly adapt to modern criminal tactics. SWAT teams now handle snipers, high risk search and arrest warrants, barricaded suspects, hostage situations, and dignitary protection. Generally, if there is a situation where a suspect is believed to be armed and the incident is not resolved immediately then the SWAT team will get the call.

Some police departments use their SWAT teams for more common police patrol as in drug warrant searches, street stops of suspected gang members, and routine patrol in high-crime neighborhoods. The use of SWAT teams in this capacity has received criticism from citizens and people from the criminal justice academic arena. Their complaints are that SWAT teams are too military looking and the common site of these units could wear away the public perception of the police as public servant. Another problem for SWAT teams is the misconception that they are too willing to use force since they have a lot of weapons that normal police do not use. The truth is that SWAT teams often de-escalate a situation, avoiding the use-of-force option, and instead they employ less-than-lethal weapons as much as officer safety allows. There is a fine line that each police department walks to protect and

serve its citizens while practicing officer safety and yet keep from becoming a police state.

SWAT team members are volunteers from the ranks of their department. When SWAT teams have an opening, all members of the department with the required time in service (usually three to four years is the minimum) that want to be a member, regardless of sex, may apply to go through the selection process. This process includes a physical fitness test, firearms qualifications, and oral interviews to whether the candidate is of serious mind and conviction for the position. The top scores are then evaluated and submitted to the team for consideration.

Once the new members are selected for the team they go through extensive training in operational tactics and high-risk entry techniques. Each member is trained in the use of the specialized weapons that the SWAT team employs. Members are assigned a role in the team that will require them to be an expert with all designated weapons for that role. However, each officer will also be trained to use all weapons and tactics to include the combat shotgun, the submachine gun, the use of chemical agents, distraction devices and counter sniper training.

SWAT teams are usually on call twenty-four hours a day for any and all emergencies. Since they never know what situation they will respond to next, training is the

Above: These members of the SWAT team perform a search and rescue of a building. Notice how the last member of the team guards the rear just in case someone is sneaking up from behind. *Photograph courtesy of Leslie O'Shaughnessy Studios*

POLICE EQUIPMENT

90

Left: A SWAT team uses an old bus to practice a rescue. *Photograph courtesy of Heckler & Koch, Inc.*

Far Left: A SWAT team provides cover for an officer who is attaching a hook and cable to the bars on the window. Once the hook is attached, the vehicle will drive off and pull the bars off. *Photograph courtesy of Heckler & Koch, Inc.*

Below: Smoke and incendiary devices stun and distract suspects giving the SWAT team extra moments and a better chance at securing the scene. *Photograph courtesy of Heckler & Koch, Inc.*

Above: A member of a SWAT team readies to fire a smoke grenade from his M203-Pl 40mm grenade launcher. One use for smoke is that it can block the suspect's view of police actions.
Photograph courtesy of NICO Pyrotechnik

Right: For forced entry into houses with metal protective gates a SWAT team can use a tactical breaching torch to cut through the metal. Note on the back of the officer on the far right are other tools like a hook to pull metal bars down and bolt cutters for other locks.
Photograph courtesy of Broco, Inc.

most important ingredient to a safe and successful SWAT team. SWAT teams normally train on monthly or bi-monthly schedules and physical fitness tests every six months to a year to ensure peak performance.

Normal armament for a SWAT team are submachine guns, rifles for the counter sniper team, entry shotguns (shorter barrel) and combat shotguns (longer barrel that may/may not be pump loaded or semi-automatic), duty pistols, 37/40 mm gas launchers. The weapons may be outfitted with accessories like laser guided sights to aid in accuracy and pressure activated light switches to illuminate the dark.

The color and style of SWAT uniform is the choice of the department, with most city police agencies opting for all black in color to better blend in with night operations, while more urban jurisdictions sometimes use military type camouflage or all green uniforms. Even though all uniforms are made to blend into their surroundings as much as possible they still will be emblazoned with "Police" or "Sheriff" to properly identify the officer.

The special equipment that a SWAT team carries depends on the unit. SWAT teams usually wear tactical body armor that provides more protection than the soft body armor worn by most patrol officers. The

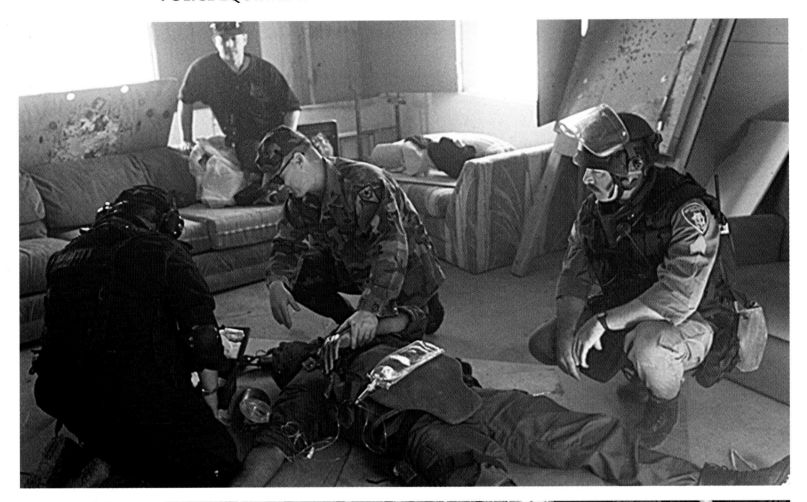

Above and Right: A lot of SWAT teams are incorporating trained medics into theor squads so that medical attention can be administered sooner to suspects, victims, and officers. *Photograph courtesy of Heckler & Koch, Inc.*

Left: These officers use pressure activated flashlights attached to their weapons to allow them to conduct a room search in no-light conditions. *Photograph courtesy of Heckler & Koch, Inc.*

Left: For a quicker reload this officer has taped another magazine of ammunition to his first one so that he can instantly insert the new one. *Photograph courtesy of Heckler & Koch, Inc.*

Right: These SWAT team officers ascend the stairs keeping a watchful eye for what is both above and below them. Notice the bullet resistant shield carried has the insignia of the Police Department clearly emblazoned on the front so that criminals will know exactly who is coming. No one can claim they did not know it was the police behind the shield later in court. *Photograph courtesy of Leslie O'Shaughnessy Studios*

extra protection is determined by the style of body armor that the officer wants to wear, for instance there are additional armor protection possibilities for the neck, groin, and other parts of the body in addition to optional hard-armor plates that can be inserted or worn on top of existing vests. The officers understand that the more armor protection that is worn, the more weight and less maneuverability they will have to carry out their mission. With the armor, the SWAT officer also has a helmet and optional face shield attachment. If the helmet does not have a face shield the officer will probably wear goggles which are worn to protect the officer's eyes from flying objects and debris kicked up when diversionary devices and the like are used. SWAT officers often employ a ballistic shield that is carried by the lead officer. These shields normally weigh around 30lbs and have a small viewing port for the officer to see through as they advance. The ballistic shield offers mobile protection from large caliber weapons. SWAT teams often carry gas masks for use when chemical weapons are deployed and to help them breath if there is smoke from a fire.

Extra equipment to aid in a forced entry are the battering ram, the many styles of grappling hooks, tactical breaching torches, and diversionary devices. The battering rams come in various sizes which all depends on the manufacturers. A battering ram will have two handles that the officer uses to swing the heavy bar and crash the ram next to the door's lock/handle. The concentration of force usually defeats the locking mechanism in the first or second attempt and allows the SWAT officers quick entry to a house. For metal bars on windows or doors the SWAT officers have various hooks to pull or torches to cut through the metal. Diversionary devices are less-than-lethal grenades that create a bright flash and/or a loud bang that is meant to disorient and stun the suspect and allow the SWAT team to enter and disable a situation safely.

SWAT teams incorporate specialists into a cohesive group. SWAT teams often train with medics, hostage negotiators, and members of the bomb squad to be prepared for emergencies that need their skills. Training is the key for this unit since their lives depend on the skilled reactions and trust of their peers.

Above: This SWAT team swoops in to make the arrest. Notice how the officers cover all aspects of the car in case there was a second, hidden suspect and yet keep from getting in a crossfire with each other.
Photograph courtesy of the Sure-Fire Institute

Right: The battering ram is used to open locked doors and give police quicker access. The ram has two handles that the officer uses to swing the heavy bar, concentrating the force at a single point to break the lock. *Photograph courtesy of Heckler & Koch, Inc.*

Below: Not all SWAT operations happen in urban areas. Dangerous individuals often seek shelter in the woods or have their hideout far from civilization. *Photograph courtesy of Heckler & Koch, Inc.*

CHAPTER THREE

Radios & Computers

"It was 1932 when the Philadelphia Police Department installed the first one-way radio into a cruiser. In 1940, the first two-way radio was installed."

Before the invention of the two-way radio, police officers had a difficult time communicating with each other and police headquarters. Officers were especially vulnerable in dangerous situations since calling for back up was difficult or non-existent. To help lessen this vulnerability, police were outfitted with noisemakers to alert the attention of other officers in the area to respond to the emergency. Whistles, bells, and rattles were standard police equipment before the

hand-held mobile radio (as seen in the photographs in this section) was introduced.

In the early 1930s, the one-way radio was invented which allowed headquarters to call individual police cars. The one-way radio was heavy and required too much power to be carried by hand and was therefore limited to cruisers and motorcycles. A couple of years later the two-way radio was invented which finally allowed officers to talk back and forth with headquarters in order to update their situations and status. The two-way radio was a leap forward in officer safety but it still was not small enough to be hand-held. When officers left their cruisers they effectively cut off their communication link to headquarters.

By the time the Korean War took place, U.S. military personnel were using hand-held two-way radios. The radio was very large being close to eighteen inches long and several pounds compared to modern standards. Due to its size, this new radio was too large for law enforcement purposes and it was not until years later that a lightweight truly mobile two-way radio was manufactured for police purposes.

The modern compact radios come with re-chargeable/replaceable batteries and are capable of sending and receiving transmissions on many different channels. Police departments have multiple channels because of the different operations that need to be conducted at the same time. For instance, vice narcotics may need one channel for a sting operation while the SWAT team will need another for a hostage crises, and normal operations will always have their own. Radios may also be mounted on

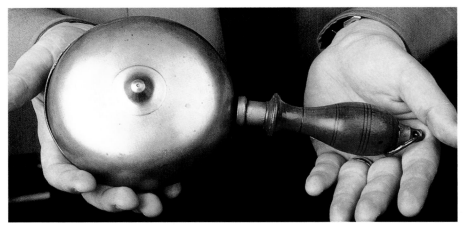

Far Left, Above: Before the hand-held radio, officers would carry a bell that they could ring in order to alert other officers to their location and to emergencies.

Far Left, Below: Another method of communication was the rattle. Officers would twirl this rattle to make a loud enough noise to be heard over the noise of busy city streets.

Left: This officer is using an ear piece and throat micro-phone to maintain hands-free communication in tactical environments. This device is used when officers do not want the suspects to hear them talk to each other.
Photograph courtesy of Television Equipment Associates

POLICE EQUIPMENT

Right: The modern mobile radio revolutionized the way police performed their duties. Now the officer can go almost anywhere and still be in instant contact with headquarters and other police units.

the officer's belt with an extension microphone connection leading to the shoulder. This makes it easier for the officer to hear and transmit without encumbering their hands.

Computers have come a long way in a short time. Just twenty years ago there were almost no computers used by patrol officers. By 1993, 6% of cruisers had car-mounted mobile digital terminals and 67% of all police departments were using some form of a computer to perform their duties. For police that have the car-mounted digital terminals they are allowed to perform wanted checks on suspects, vehicles, and send and receive messages with headquarters and other officers. Officers are now testing a system that will allow them to take a picture of a suspect and send the photograph to another officer to verify information.

Right: The two-way radio revolutionized the way police could serve the public. Officers could stay in constant contact with each other and headquarters and thus more aggressively pursue criminals.
Photograph courtesy of Leslie O'Shaughnessy Studios

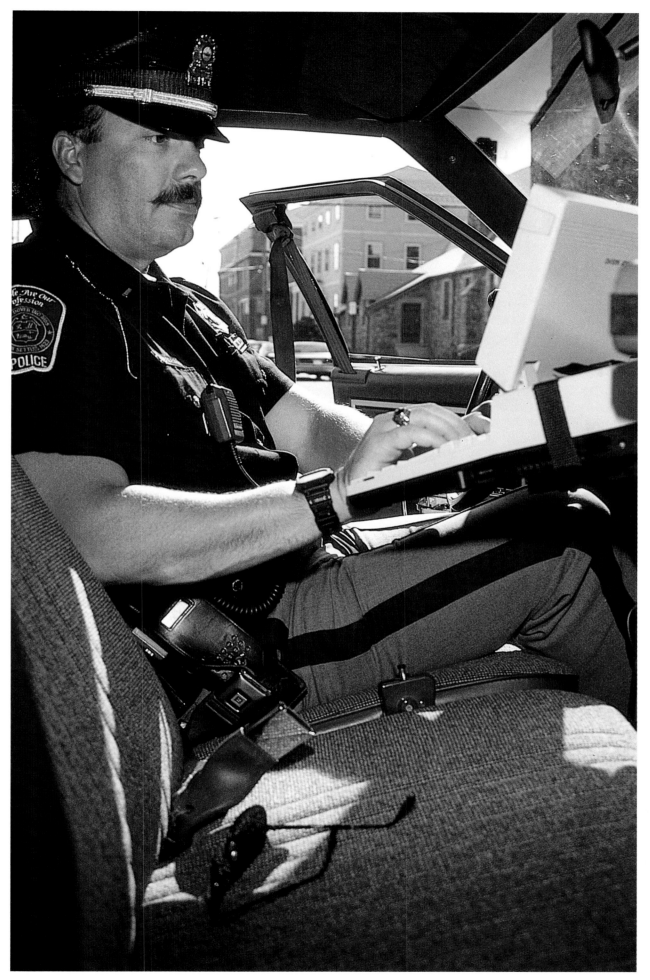

Left: Officers that have mobile digital monitors can perform wanted checks on people, automobiles, and property right from their cruiser. *Photograph courtesy of Leslie O'Shaughnessy Studios*

103

CHAPTER THREE

K9

*"Less than 1% of a job a dog does involves its' mouth.
More than 99% involves its' nose."*
Jim Watson, North American Police Work Dog Association.

Below: K-9 officers and their partners often find themselves in dangerous situations. Bullet resistant vests are made to fit the dog that allow for free movement along with protection of some of the vital areas.
Photograph courtesy of 21st Century Hard Armor Protection, Inc.

As soon as dogs were domesticated by man, they have been trained to perform services for their master. However, the possibilities of canine (K-9) services were limited, not by the dog, but by man's understanding of the dog's potential. Initially, canines provided companionship and assisted in guard and hunting duties. Over time man discovered that the dog could guard sheep and other domesticated animals alone, not only due to their obviously keener sense of hearing and smell but also their intense loyalty.

In the early 1900s, the first police dog started service in the United States. Since then the use of police dogs has ballooned to more than 8,000 dogs working the streets today. The explosion of canine use has occurred rather recently due to the fact that man has begun to realize that the dog is much smarter and more capable than they were initially given credit. Police dogs can be trained to sniff for a variety of scents, including ingredients used to make bombs, narcotics of almost all types, as well as individual people. In addition to being trained to track individual people, dogs are also being trained to find people in case they are buried under a collapsed or exploded building or under the snow caused by an avalanche.

The dog's sense of smell is much greater than human beings. Dogs can sniff the air and pick up a scent with only five parts per billion of the material present, which is about 1,000 times better than humans. Drug smugglers have tried all sorts of hiding tricks to keep their narcotics from being detected, but the dog has been consistently able to expose these secret-hiding places. The best scent-detection technology that man possesses today is far inferior to dogs ability to detect a scent.

Not every dog can be used for police service. Dogs, like people, are not always suited for police work. Police dogs have to have the ability to be both approachable by the public and aggressive when needed. Gun shots and stressful situations cannot adversely affect the dog from carrying out it's mission. The normal activities that each police dog must endure can be very tough, making a police K-9 a valuable asset to the force.

Left: The K-9 partner can hear better than their human counterpart which is very helpful at night. Here, a K-9 has alerted this officer to something hiding in the dark. The officer uses the light attached to her service weapon to help her see what her companion sees. *Photograph courtesy of Surefire Institute*

Above and Inset Right: People outside of the law enforcement community rarely realize that police dogs receive their own badge and identification. You can clearly see the name of the dog, "Santo" is at the bottom of the badge.

Right: Some police dogs are specially trained to find explosives. Their sensitive noses can detect and trace even small amounts of explosives. In this photo, the police dog is searching buses for hidden bombs before a special event. *Photograph courtesy of the San Francisco Police Department*

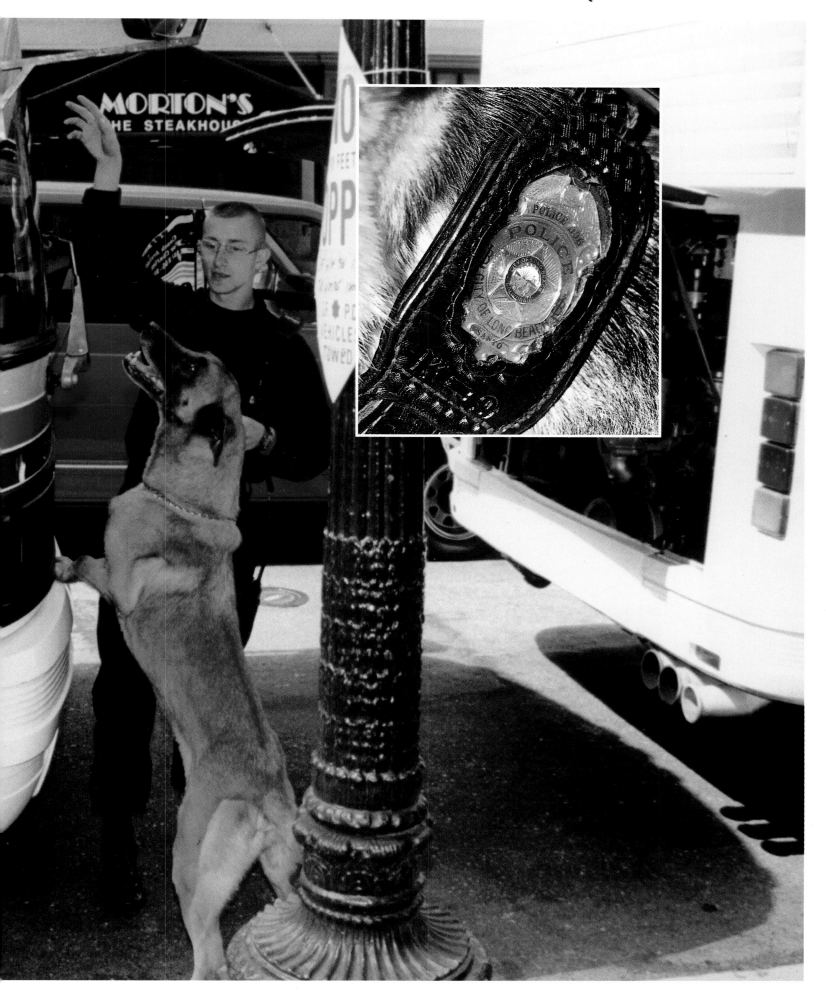

CHAPTER THREE

Scuba Diving

"Roughly 7-9% of evidence is gathered on the water as compared to evidence gathered on land."
Colonel Dean Royer Vice President Marine Patrol Association

Most Police Departments have a body of water somewhere in their jurisdiction. Rivers, lakes, ponds, and any other bodies of water too deep for officers to wade in or see to the bottom pose possible emergency or criminal evidentiary situations. Police Departments have to be prepared for these situations and police scuba divers respond every day.

Since there is not enough need for a full-time scuba diver in most Police Departments, police scuba divers are called on to dive in addition to their regular duties. Most police scuba divers receive their diving certificate as a result of their own personal interest in recreation diving or as a member of a Police Department's marine

patrol unit they need one (only jurisdictions with a large body of water will have a marine patrol unit.) To be certified as a police scuba diver they must undergo an intensive training seminar on topics related to police work, such as retrieval of evidence and the complexities of conducting an underwater search. Police divers do not carry their equipment with them in their cruiser for safety reasons, but the scuba gear is always ready at headquarters for emergencies.

Police divers usually perform two types of service: water rescue or evidence gathering.

Water rescue is typically done with other agencies such as the coast guard or fire department. Police scuba divers usually

Right: Police scuba divers pull a pistol used in a crime out of a lake. Evidence gathering and handling is very important for court so the diver is seen here putting the gun in a plastic container to be properly kept.
Photo courtesy of Leslie O'Shaughnessy studios

Left: Typical police scuba diving equipment. In the picture can be seen: a Viking dry suit, 40lb weight belt, underwater light, flippers, gloves, 60cu in air tank (giving 45-60 minutes of air), Aga full-face positive pressure diving mask, pattern line in the yellow bag, buoy, and compass.

assist the other agencies who specialize in such operations. The police scuba divers will normally take the lead in a rescue if they are the first on the scene or if there is a crime still in progress.

It is a common criminal activity to dispose of evidence in a body of water since the probability of it being discovered is drastically reduced. Thus, evidence gathering is the most common task for the police scuba diver. For example, like the movies, criminals often throw the gun used in a crime off a bridge. In doing this, the criminal not only hides evidence, but also effectively washes the fingerprints off a gun. However, with the

use of police divers, the recovered gun can reveal ample evidence for conviction. The gun's serial number can prove ownership and the ballistic signature (the telltale grooves the soft lead of a bullet gets from the rifling of the barrel) can be used to connect the gun to the actual bullet from the crime scene.

Because the handling of evidence is an important part of a criminal prosecution and would entail testifying in a court of law, police departments want their own officers or fellow officers from other jurisdictions conducting the search for evidence and not a civilian diver.

CHAPTER THREE

Bomb Squad Equipment

The Explosive Ordnance Device (EOD) Unit, or the Bomb Squad as they are most often called, is a highly trained law enforcement team of police volunteers that is becoming a necessary part of police duties more and more often. Not every jurisdiction will have an EOD unit. Mostly large cities/counties, State police, and Federal agencies will spend the money required to adequately support the unit.

A typical bomb squad consists of at least four officers that are trained to render safe the many different bombs that they might come in contact. These officers are often called bomb technicians and must go through rigorous training at the Hazardous Devices School in Alabama to be ready for this dangerous job. This training facility is the only school in the United States that trains public safety officials as bomb

Right: See how the trailer being towed has a container. This is where bombs are placed for transport. The cylinder has no top so the blast will be directed harmlessly upwards. The towing vehicle transports the bomb disposal unit and holds all the gear for the squad. *Photograph courtesy of Leslie O'Shaughnessy Studios*

Left: Officers of the Explosive Ordnance Device Unit (bomb squad) suit-up with special protective armor that provides protection against blast, fragmentation, and heat from an explosive device. When all dressed the officer will be covered from head to toe with as much as 45lbs of protective clothing.
Photograph courtesy of Leslie O'Shaughnessy Studios

Below: Remotely operated bomb disposal robots can have saws attached to them so that they can get at explosive devices in vans, cars, and the like.
Photograph courtesy of Engineering Technology Incorporated.

disposal technicians. Over 5,000 technicians have graduated from the basic course and 4,000 have received refresher training since 1981. Usually, the bomb squad is backed-up by K9 officers and their partners that are trained to sniff for bombs.

The equipment used for this job varies but the standards are a truck to contain all the necessary render safe equipment, bomb disposal robot, bomb protective suits, screening (X-ray machine, and other equipment) and disruption equipment. Bomb disposal suits are similar to the bullet resistant vests worn by regular patrol officers but these cover much more of the body. These suits are heavy and when the officer is completely outfitted the total weight can be over 45lbs yet they are built to provide ease of movement for the officers and the delicate work they perform. The suit is made to protect against blast, fragmentation, and heat

Above and Right:
Explosive Ordnance
Device Unit robots
are strong, remote
operated machines
that can be tether,
fiber optic, or wire-
less controlled. These
robots can get
through tough terrain
to perform a job that
would threaten
human lives.
*Photographs courtesy
of Northrop
Grumman
Corporation*

"There were 5,196 explosive incidents reported to or investigated by the Bureau of Alcohol, Tobacco and Firearms in 1995."
Bureau of Alcohol, Tobacco and Firearms.

from an explosive device. Bomb disposal robots are used to handle the explosive devices from a safe distance using extremely sensitive remote controls and video feed back. Screening equipment like X-ray machines help the bomb technicians see through packages to help determine what a bomb is made of or to verify if it really is a bomb. Disruption equipment is used to destroy the bomb or parts of the bomb without setting off the explosion from the bomb itself.

The bomb has become a weapon of choice for criminals that want to kill people or destroy property. Significant advances in bomb making technology and fuzing systems have made some bombs very small and tough to detect, for instance the Unabomber used small bombs placed in packages to be mailed. While other criminals are using more common ingredients to make enormous bombs that take out whole buildings like the Oklahoma City bombing. Bombers often choose targets at random and

evade law enforcement by the remote nature of the crime.

Bomb squads also have a retrieval-transport trailer that is towed to the situation. The retrieval-transport trailer consists of a cylindrical tube where a bomb can be placed and towed to a safer location to be rendered safe. The tube has no top so that if the explosive device were to prematurely explode before being rendered safe then the blast will be directed upwards, not outwards and hopefully cause less damage to people and property.

The bomb squad also provides a public service to the community since they often provide bomb threat awareness programs for other police departments and private corporations.

Please remember that only certain pictures and information were used in the publishing of this book since the techniques and strategies used to defeat the bombs criminals make in our society is quite secret.

Below Left: An armored personnel carrier can provide a lot of portable protection to the bomb technician.
Photograph courtesy of Thomas Lynch

Below: The armored personnel carrier also can transport the extra equipment the bomb technician might need.
Photograph courtesy of Thomas Lynch

CHAPTER THREE

Mounted Unit Equipment

Police equestrian units ceased being the most common form of transportation for law enforcement with the advent of the motorcycle and the automobile. Due to the high cost of upkeep and the inability of the horse to keep pace with a speeding car, most police jurisdictions stopped using the mounted officer altogether. Even cities synonymous with cowboys and the west, like Fort Worth, Texas stopped using the horse to aid the officer on patrol.

However, with the increase in public protests during the late 1960s and early 70s, police departments started to see the benefit in having a special squad of mounted police and more and more equestrian units have been established since the 70s. The new popularity of the mounted units was not for their ability to transport the officer, but for their assistance in riot and crowd control. An added benefit came with the good public relations boost the mounted officer gave each department.

If a crowd begins to become unruly, the officer on horseback can see over the masses of people and help direct law enforcement activities aimed at dispersing the crowd. Conversely, people can see the

Right: On the beach, a mounted officer can see much more from his position. In addition, the horse is trained to not step on anyone so there poses little risk to the large number of beachgoers and children. Note how the mounted officer uses the long straight baton rather than the side-handle or the expandable baton because those batons would not reach the target. *Photograph courtesy of Leslie O'Shaughnessy Studios*

Left: In riot or crowd control situations, even the horse needs protection. Here a horse wears armor for the vulnerable nose and a plexi-glass eye shield for protection.
Photo courtesy of Mounted Police Training & Equipment Co.

Right: A little more than a hundred years ago the police of New York City depended on the horse as the only mode of transportation to get around the city quickly. Now, the horse has few, but important assignments and patrol duties.

mounted officer in a crowd from a greater distance. Once people can see the officer, their likelihood of committing a crime will lesson since they know they stand a greater chance of getting caught, thus the mounted officer is a better deterrent to crime. Although crowd control training and performance is very demanding to both horse and rider, it is an invaluable advantage to have several hundred pounds of animal to help people from becoming unruly.

The mounted units are also especially useful in searching rugged terrain for lost persons. This is because horses can cover a greater distance in a shorter amount of time than humans can. Furthermore, officers can see more from their vantage point atop a horse than they can walking on the ground. The biggest but least quantifiable benefit comes from the good public relations that the horse and rider bring to children and adults when they come in contact.

CHAPTER FOUR

Surveillance & Forensic Tools

Left: This officer is using his most utilized tool, the notepad. The officer collects information from a wide range of sources everyday to monitor activity in his or her patrol area. *Photograph courtesy of the San Francisco Police Department*

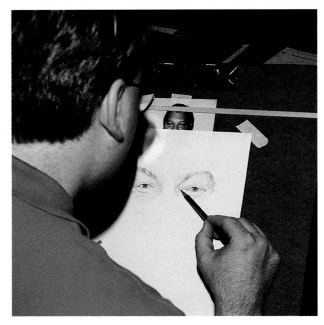

The major responsibility of crime scene investigators is to reconstruct what happened at a crime scene so that it will be possible for them to identify the responsible parties. To solve and prosecute a crime, the investigator needs to recognize and properly collect the physical evidence left at the scene. The first step investigators perform is to secure the crime scene so that evidence is not inadvertently destroyed and then to carefully document the conditions at the scene and identify all relevant physical evidence.

Proper crime scene investigation is a difficult and time-consuming process. The investigator must be methodical in the collection of evidence and use his prior investigative experiences to know what to look for at the scene. Making sure not to arrive at any hasty conclusions, the investigator must determine several different theories of the crime using only the physical evidence and keeping only the scenarios not eliminated by the evidence.

In documenting the crime scene, the investigator relies on other police officers to gather evidence, identification technicians to take photographs and fingerprints, and witnesses of the crime to provide their account of the crime. Once all of the evidence is collected the investigator will rely on laboratory technicians at the various crime laboratories and doctors at the coroner's office for expert evaluation of the evidence.

Little details can sometimes explain much more than one might think, especially at homicide investigations. Some of the small details that were later used to help solve cases are: the position that the lights were left (on or off), the persons vehicle was missing while their keys remained, and a different product brand was found which was not typically used by the person in question. Some evidence is much more fragile than others and has to be collected immediately such as shoeprints, tire tread imprints, and gunshot residue.

Items left by the suspects in the crime are always excellent clues. Remember that the purpose of the evidence gathered by the investigator is to connect the crime to the suspect. Often when criminals are in a haste or have to struggle to get away they drop their wallets or leave the tools used in the burglary like screwdrivers or ski masks. It is important for the investigator to determine what is out of place in order to find this type of evidence. The investigator searches for anything that the criminal might have left behind or accidentally disturbed during the crime since fingerprints and footprints will be found in those areas. Other evidence left by the suspect may not be so obvious such as hairs or microscopic particles left behind or taken by the suspect.

CHAPTER FOUR

Polygraph

A polygraph machine, often called a lie-detector test, collects physiological data from at least three areas of the human body. Rubber tubes are placed over the examinee's chest and abdomen to record respiratory activity. Two metal plates are attached to the fingers to record sweat gland activity and a blood pressure cuff or similar device records cardiovascular activity.

The polygraph examiner will ask standard questions that are easily answered truthfully like the examinee's age and sex to use as a standard of measurement against possible untruths. The examiner will then ask the questions that are unknown to gauge the examinee's reaction. Certain guidelines are followed to determine truthful answers to false ones.

The polygraph test is a tool for law enforcement that a suspect does not have to take nor is it currently admissible in court. There is an ongoing controversy of the validity of the test and whether people are able to lie to the machine without being detected. Still, the polygraph test is used by a lot of police departments because it has proved effective more times than not to narrow the number of suspects down in an investigation.

Left: The polygraph machine measures respiratory, sweat gland, and blood pressure activity to determine the reactions of the examinee. Truthful reactions are compared to questions of unknown truth to gauge the honesty of the examinee. *Photograph courtesy of Leslie O'Shaughnessy Studios*

CHAPTER FOUR

Fingerprints

"Fingerprinting was first used in America in 1902. The FBI was the first law enforcement agency to use D.N.A testing methods to solve crimes in 1988."

On everyone's skin there are very small sweat pores that are constantly exuding perspiration. This perspiration adheres to the outline of the ridges of our fingerprints. Other substances, like oil from touching your face and hair also adhere to these ridges. A recording of your fingerprint or palmprint is typically left on the surface of most objects that you touch. Sometimes the print is clearly visible, like on a window pane, but most of the time the invisible fingerprint must be developed or made visible either by the application of powders, chemicals or electronic means.

When a police identification technician is trying to lift a fingerprint off a surface they often use powders as seen in the pictures in this section. Different powders are used for different surfaces. Magnetic powder is recommended for use in dusting glossy surfaces such as plastics, magazine covers, and tissue paper. Fluorescent powders are for pebble-grained dashboards and textured surfaces while colored powders, like black, silver, and white, are for the more common application on glass, metals, and most guns. Special brushes are used to apply the different powders, which allow a thin layer of powder to touch the ridges of the fingerprint. If a technician adds too much powder, the whole print will be filled in and ruined. Once the powder has been applied and the fingerprint is visible the technician lifts the print using clear tape.

Right: This police lab technician is looking for fingerprints on this rifle using powder to bring out faint features.
Photograph courtesy of Lightning Powder Company, Inc.

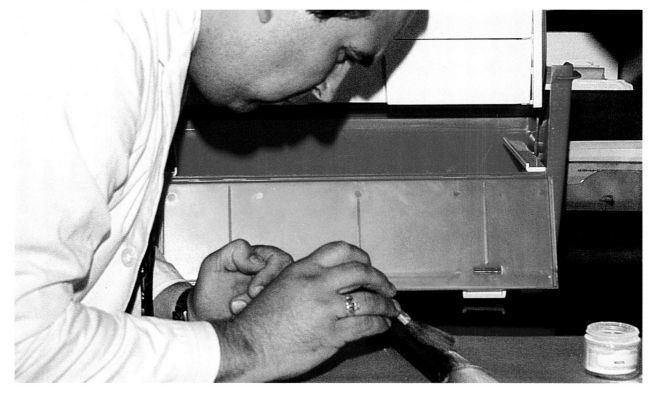

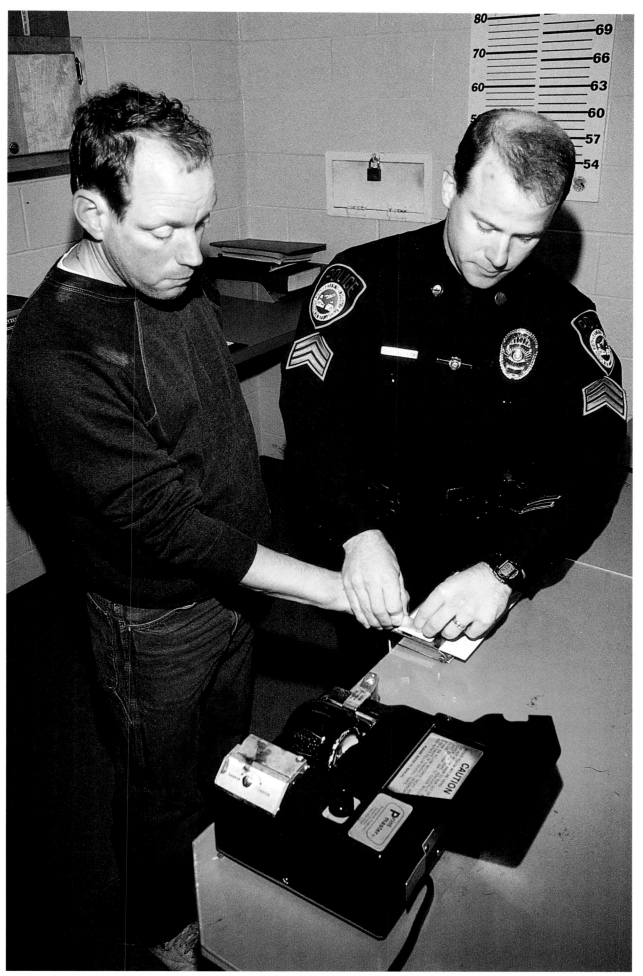

Left: When someone is arrested they are taken to the booking room where they are fingerprinted and photographed. Each finger, thumb, and palm print is put on a card to be indexed and filed where they can be matched against crime scene latent prints. Today, these prints are stored electronically and can be viewed nationwide by most law enforcement agencies.
Photograph courtesy of Leslie O'Shaughnessy Studios

121

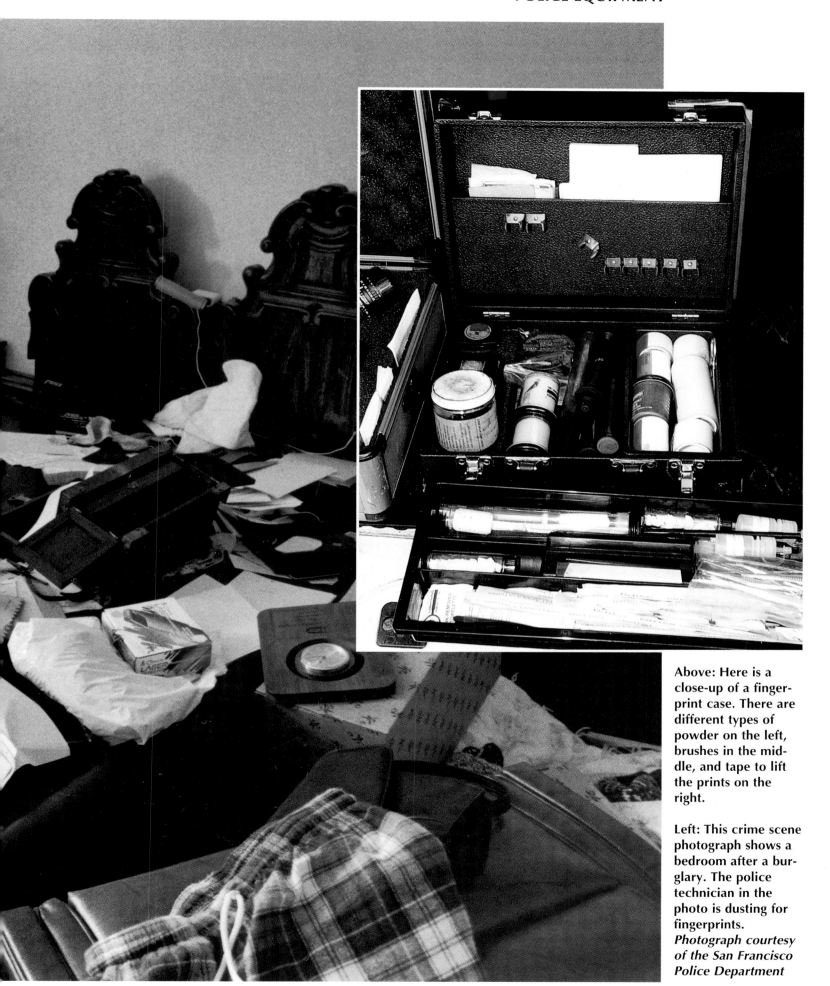

Above: Here is a close-up of a fingerprint case. There are different types of powder on the left, brushes in the middle, and tape to lift the prints on the right.

Left: This crime scene photograph shows a bedroom after a burglary. The police technician in the photo is dusting for fingerprints. *Photograph courtesy of the San Francisco Police Department*

CHAPTER FOUR

Traffic Accidents

"Approximately 1.5 million drivers were arrested in 1996 for driving under the influence of alcohol or narcotics. This is an arrest rate of 1 for every 122 licensed drivers in the United States."

Below: Accident investigation is a science where good investigators apply math, motor mechanics, and witness testimony to reconstruct the scene. *Photograph courtesy of Leslie O'Shaughnessy Studios*

All officers are taught the basics of accident reconstruction and the traffic laws that govern the road. For serious accidents and hit-and-run investigations most police departments train some officers to become certified accident investigation experts. This is a specialized science where officers are schooled in trigonometry, geometry, algebra, and calculus as those disciplines relate to motor vehicles. Officers learn about auto mechanics, evidence gathering techniques,

and a more thorough knowledge of the applicable traffic laws to enhance their ability to conduct such investigations.

Driving under the influence (DUI) of alcohol or narcotics is a major problem for the safety of the public. For the last 20 years that data has been collected on fatalities in alcohol related crashes, 40-55% of all motor vehicle fatalities have been alcohol related. Since there are few items of equipment that can assist an officer in DUI traffic stops, law

Left: Officers often stop drivers for other traffic violations like speeding or running a red, only to discover that the driver is actually intoxicated. This officer uses the radar gun to monitor traffic; he must be careful to only record the speed of one vehicle, keeping in mind that radar waves spread out over distance. *Photograph courtesy of Leslie O'Shaughnessy Studios*

Below Left: Here is an officer administering a breath test with a hand-held analyzer. He holds his hand up to feel for the woman's breath since a common ploy of suspects is to not really blow through the testing straw. *Photograph courtesy of PJ Lepp*

Far Left: The officers are dealing with the aftermath of a serious car accident, which is unfortunately a common occurrence that occupies a significant portion of a department's resources. *Photograph courtesy of San Francisco Police Department*

Left: Officers use tape to measure the length of a tire skid mark. The length of the skid will help them determine the speed of the vehicle and reconstruct the accident. *Photograph courtesy of Leslie O'Shaughnessy Studios*

enforcement agencies rely largely on good police skills to get these dangerous drivers off the road. Once the police have the suspected impaired driver pulled over they can have them perform simple tests like saying the alphabet or walking a straight line to determine the level of intoxication.

A tool that is used on the street to gauge the Blood-Alcohol-Content (BAC) of a driver is a portable breath analyzer. This hand-held tool is not admissible in court because of questions about the sophistication of the equipment to gather an exact reading but it is accurate enough to let police know if the driver is over the legal limit or not. If the driver is deemed to be over the legal limit then the officer will take the driver to the police station for a court-approved BAC test of the breath by a breathalyzer machine or to have blood drawn at a local hospital.

CHAPTER FOUR

Thermal Imaging and Night Vision Equipment

Below, Left and Right: These thermal images are from a cruiser-mounted system. The officer can clearly see a suspect about to break a car window and another shows a burglar fixing to break into this home. *Photograph courtesy of Raytheon/B.E. Meyers*

More police departments are using night vision and thermal imaging equipment than ever before. Since the 1980s, the imaging equipment has become more affordable for police departments and the equipment's abilities have improved. Night vision equipment allows officers to see in the near absence of light, which is a large tactical advantage over criminals. Night vision equipment comes in several forms. For instance, there is the pocketscope that is similar to a scope on a rifle and the goggles that SWAT teams can strap to their faces so that their hands are free to accomplish their mission.

Thermal imaging cameras use infrared light waves to let the officer see at night. In essence the device lets officers see the heat that is emitted by humans, animals, and machines that generate heat like automobiles. In the thermal imaging photographs provided in this section one can see the heat emanating from the suspect's face and hands but not from the street or the house

Left: Night vision goggles can be attached to the face securely (the officer can quickly swivel them up and out of his face if need be). This allows an officer to have a distinct advantage over a suspect in low light conditions. *Photograph courtesy of Heckler & Koch, Inc.*

Right: Here is a view from one of the thermal images on a helicopter. If you look closely the suspect has climbed on the roof of the house and a police officer, being directed from the helicopter, is closing in.
Photograph courtesy of Flir Systems, Inc.

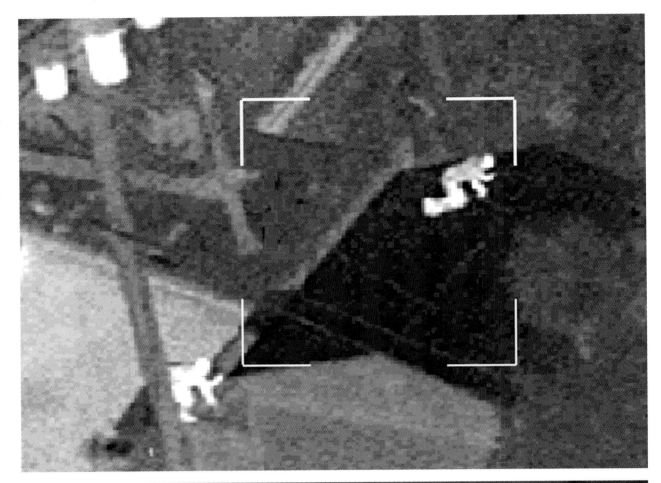

Right: The officer's view from the helicopter is surprisingly clear using thermal imaging.
Photograph courtesy of Flir Systems, Inc.

CHAPTER FIVE

Police Equipment of the Future

Left: This officer is loaded with a state of the art kit. Today, developments in communications, weapons, transport, and forensics make the police force more effective than it has ever been in the past. And further improvements are always being made to keep the force one step ahead of the criminals.

Right: Tomorrow's officers will be able to send and receive photos and video imagery to aid in identifying suspects, clearing warrants, and recording video evidence. Combining videos and photos with modern communications technology will allow officers to quickly share information with the rest of the department. *Photograph courtesy of Kenwood Communications*

Law enforcement techniques and equipment are constantly evolving to incorporate new technologies. New inventions and improvements of existing police equipment help the police better monitor criminal behavior that is also becoming more sophisticated. New police tactics are being developed to handle situations in a manner that meets changes that have occurred in public opinion.

The police equipment of tomorrow is developed from many sources. Sometimes, police officers themselves see modern equipment used for other functions and decide to adapt it to meet their enforcement needs. One instance of this is the introduction of mountain bikes in neighborhood patrols. When scientists invent new products or enhance existing products that can be used in law enforcement like night vision devices they include police departments as potential buyers.

In addition, more and more future police equipment is coming through partnerships with the U.S. Departments of Justice and Defense. Since the U.S. military is being deployed to perform an increased number of peacekeeping missions that require less-than-lethal options, new technology is being researched and developed for them. The U.S. Marines used sticky-foam in Somalia and the U.S. Army used foam batons, sponge grenades and 40mm rubber bullets in situations in Haiti and Bosnia. These new

less-than-lethal options proved successful in controlling unruly situations while incurring the minimum risk to human life. Furthermore, less-than-lethal technologies are the most welcomed advance in law enforcement by the general public. Due to the success of less-than-lethal technologies in a military setting, civilian law enforcement agencies are now able to procure these new technologies for their officers to use in civilian situations.

One of the most noticeable modern advances is the computer. Not only are computers getting more powerful and faster, they are also getting smaller which makes them a better tool for the future of law enforcement applications. Today's technology is on the verge of allowing an officer to capture an image of a suspicious individual, check it against a computer database stored miles away for outstanding warrants and past criminal activity. If the individual is wanted for a crime, their image could be sent to by one officer's cruiser to other officers on patrol in that area. Computers and communications technology is currently being developed and tested to help officers collaborate with investigators, social workers, and prosecutors to proactively prevent crime. Correspondingly, computer systems are being field tested to assist in planning and deploying police assets to match patterns of criminal activity so that more crimes are prevented.

CHAPTER FIVE

Less-Than-Lethal Weapons

Most police work is done through communication. A police officer's main goal is to talk to all of the people involved in a situation and resolve any conflicts or misunderstandings through speaking, using force only when all other options fail. Officers are trained to use force as sparingly as possible and use deadly force as an absolutely final resort. The newest tactic of law enforcement is focusing on less-than-lethal options as a means of reducing the already limited need to use deadly force. Notable cases like the Branch Davidian stand-off in Waco, Texas that ended with tremendous loss of life might not have been as tragic if officers had the option of these new, less-than-lethal options.

Another police situation that has benefited from the introduction of less-than-lethal options is in riot control. Riots have always posed a problem for police. The problem is how to establish order from an unruly mob without using deadly force to achieve that goal. Tear gas and spraying water have been used since the early 60s with success but often with the disapproval of general public opinion and some injuries to the rioters. The new less-then-lethal equipment such as less-

Left: Currently, pepper spray is dispensed from an aerosol container with an effectiveness of two to six feet. This type of delivery means that the officer must be very close to the suspect when using the pepper spray. Now being tested are pepper powder or spray projectiles in the form of paint balls. Using conventional paint ball launchers the balls of pepper powder or spray can be fired up to 100 feet away. *Photograph courtesy of Jaycor*

Top Right: In a typical scenario, an unruly individual by himself or in a crowd can be shot with this less-than-lethal pepper powder or spray ball at chest level from a safe distance. The man in this photograph is being shot with pepper spray balls at 30 feet and subdued without subjecting the officer to harm.
Photograph courtesy of Jaycor

Middle Right: This dummy was shot with a pepper powder ball that produced a cloud of pepper dust around the dummy's nose, mouth, and eyes where the pepper will have the most affect.
Photograph courtesy of Jaycor

Below Right: Police have been using stun guns and tasers for years to deliver less-than-lethal electrical shocks to subdue unruly individuals who are extremely violent. To use the stun gun or taser the officer must be at a distance of no less than 12 feet. Currently, a new device is being tested to effectively electrically stun a person at a far greater distance than available now to improve officer safety. This photograph shows the electrical round coming out of the gun.
Photograph courtesy of Jaycor

than-lethal grenades that explode rubber shrapnel and "paint balls" that can deliver a small amount of pepper spray or powder to a specific individual rather than whole crowd. New less-than-lethal equipment being developed uses ultra-sonic waves in an acoustic gun that sends focused waves of sound that will disrupt rioters stomachs to make them nauseous, but cause no permanent damage.

Armed standoffs are not the only situations that police can use less-than-lethal tactics and equipment. Vehicle pursuits often cause the death of civilians, criminals, and the police. New ways to disable a vehicle are being developed to allow police to stop a vehicle in a more controlled and safer manner than available today. Currently, less-than-lethal spikes can be deployed in the road to deflate the tires of a vehicle and slow it down with relative success. However, scientists are now trying to develop a focused electromagnetic pulse (EMP) gun that will wipe out the complex computer circuits that are used to operate today's modern vehicles forcing them to coast to a stop like they ran out of gas. The focused EMP gun could be fired from the cruiser at the fleeing vehicle without harming the passengers or civilians and make the car come to a stop.

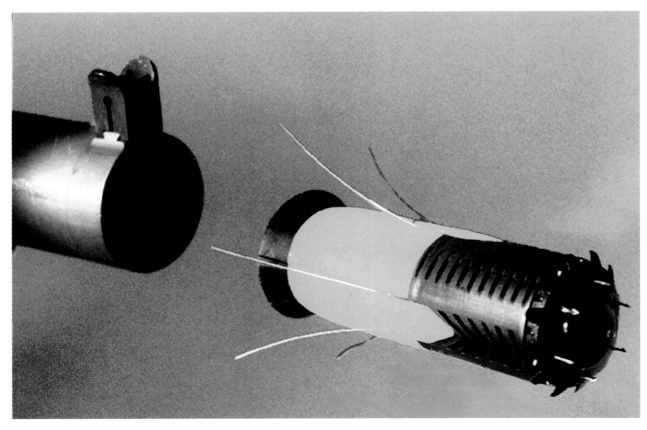

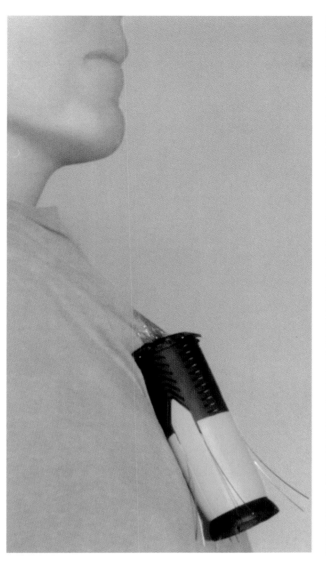

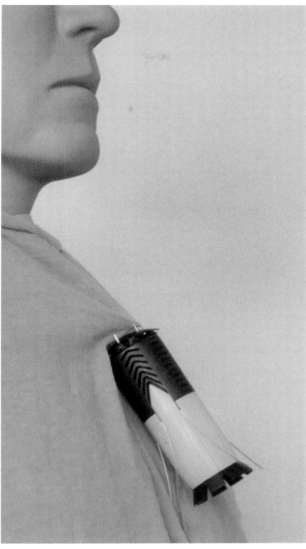

Far Left: The electrical round has three options. Shown here is the adhesive attachment. The round contains a battery pack that imparts a short burst of high-voltage pulses capable of penetrating several layers of clothing and leather.
Photograph courtesy of Jaycor

Near Left: Another form of the round is a barb for short clothing attachment and a combination adhesive/barb is in production.
Photograph courtesy of Jaycor

Left: The projectile is compatible with conventional 37/40 mm law enforcement weapons.
Photograph courtesy of Jaycor

135

CHAPTER FIVE

Transportation

Today's police departments take advantage of commercial vehicle technology and are adopting new vehicles for traditional law enforcement missions. Tomorrow's low and no exhaust electric vehicles are seeing some of their first use as police vehicles, supporting civic efforts to reduce air pollution.

Right: To combat the growing problem of high-speed vehicle pursuits a new technology uses electromagnetic pulses to disrupt a fleeing vehicle's sensitive electronics and safely stop it. The system can be either permanently employed at a location such as a border checkpoint or can be deployed in a portable manner ahead of a pursuit. As the fleeing vehicle drives over the system the electrical energy disables the vehicle's electronics without hurting the occupants of the car and brings the car to a safe, controlled stop.
Photograph courtesy of Jaycor

Left: New equipment is constantly being added to vehicles. This thermal imaging system is remotely controlled from inside the cruiser.

Left: Police transport of the future may not always rely on groundbreaking technology. The mountain bike is a quick and rugged way of getting around urban environments. In addition it does not pollute the atmosphere and even helps to keep officers fit!

CHAPTER FIVE

Other Equipment

Below Right: Some products do not always find a place in law enforcement. A researcher sprays sticky foam on a mannequin to demonstrate how corrections or police officers could use the foam to subdue an inmate or criminal suspect without bloodshed. The foam is a tenacious, tacky, non-hardening thermoplastic that would cause a suspect to stick to himself or anything he/she touches. Researchers at Sandia National Laboratories evaluated this equipment of the future to find that it was not a viable option for law enforcement.
Photo courtesy of Sandia National Laboratories, Randy Montoya photographer

New equipment to meet police officers' many various duties are plentiful and scientific developments are always throwing up more. Current development includes devices that can "see" through clothing to detect weapons and new radar and laser devices to measure vehicle speeds. In addition, advanced medical equipment such as the AED (Automated External Defibrillators), which is designed to complement CPR in saving heart attack victims, and unattended traffic monitors and remote camera systems to control areas that increase the effectiveness of scarce manpower resources will soon be available.

Not all advanced police technology is meant for use in the field. The quality of simulator training that has so greatly benefited commercial and military aviation is beginning to become available for civilian law enforcement agencies. These video and computer imagery applications are being applied to police training to quickly present officers with an ever-increasing range of scenarios before they even patrol the streets. New technology improves many aspects of the officer's job performance including the dexterity of driving in pursuits, the sensitivity of hostage situations, and decision making on whether to use lethal force.

Left: Researchers at Sandia National Laboratories have developed a suite of high-tech tools that allow bomb technicians to disable both criminal and advanced terrorist-type weapons from a safe distance. This bomb squad member sets up a remote bomb-disablement tool to "render safe" a mock suitcase bomb.
Photo courtesy of Sandia National Laboratories, Randy Montoya photographer

Above: A new product being tested by police departments is a gun that fires a 15-foot diameter net that entangles and restricts the movement of a suspect. This new piece of equipment would help police departments subdue combative subjects with minimal use of force or pain compliance. *Photograph courtesy of Foster-Miller, Inc.*

Right: Here is another view of the net entangling a person on the run. This new product is also being tested for its potential to control or neautralize threatening animals. *Photograph courtesy of Foster-Miller, Inc.*

CHAPTER FIVE

Forensic Tools

Police departments are continually employing more sophisticated laboratory techniques to assist in solving crimes. Advanced DNA processing is becoming common place and currently has the ability of making a positive identification from a microscopic sample of human tissue or fluid. Other important technologies which are employed in today's police laboratories include spectroscopy to identify chemical samples, advanced pattern matching software to more accurately match sketches with photos, and nationwide and regional databases to track criminal activity, movement, and financial activity.

Right: Researchers at Sandia National Laboratories are developing a "new evidence system" that uses the natural fluorescence and reflectance of organic matter to highlight fingerprints, semen, blood splatter, and other substances. They hope the device will allow police officers investigating a murder, rape, or other serious crime to scan a lighted crime scene with a special video camera and see evidence without the use of powders and other visual aids. *Photo courtesy of Sandia National Laboratories, Randy Montoya photographer*

Left: Now being tested is a wearable computer to be worn by police officers as they gather evidence at a crime scene. This system is a pen-based computer unit that brings together multimedia computing, laser-ranging technology and barcode tagging that allows an officer to more efficiently process complex crime scenes and reduce the potential contamination of evidence.
Photograph courtesy of Pacific Northwest National Laboratory

Right: A police crime scene technician uses an epoxy compound to make a mold of a footprint left at a crime scene. The technician can determine the suspects approximate size from the footprint and may be able to match it to the suspect's shoe. *Photograph courtesy of the San Francisco Police Department*